Praise for

A HARD KICK IN THE NUTS

"I read this book all in one sitting. I am first of all blown away by Steve-O's continued sobriety and also his honesty and complete transparency in writing this wonderful book. Eternally proud of my brother."
—Johnny Knoxville

"Thoughtful and revealing, but on-brand.... The new book is filled with profound observations and frank revelations. If the first [book] goes to the bone, this one goes to the marrow."
—*CBS Saturday Morning*

"Dude, this book is wildly engrossing. I finished it in almost three hours, and I literally hate books. Just when I thought I couldn't have seen more of Steve's private parts, he managed to bare even more stuff that most people would deny 'til their dying day. The results are riveting, hilarious, and shockingly educational."
—Whitney Cummings

"A disarmingly direct memoir of mistakes and course corrections studded with some useful advice."
—*Kirkus Reviews*

"The way Steve-O has turned his life around is just incredible. It's all in this book!"

—Dana White, President of the
Ultimate Fighting Championship

"While one might not expect to find wisdom in a hilarious tale about belly-flopping into a urine-filled kiddie pool, Glover is a veritable expert at learning 'some valuable shit from [a] lifetime of terrible decisions.' Dick jokes aside, this is full of heart and hard-won insight." —*Publishers Weekly*

A HARD
KICK
IN THE
NUTS

**Also by Stephen "Steve-O" Glover
with David Peisner**

Professional Idiot: A Memoir

A HARD KICK IN THE NUTS

WHAT I'VE LEARNED FROM A LIFETIME OF TERRIBLE DECISIONS

STEPHEN "STEVE-O" GLOVER

with **DAVID PEISNER**

hachette
BOOKS

New York

Hachette Books
Hachette Book Group
1290 Avenue of the Americas
New York, NY 10104
HachetteBooks.com
Twitter.com/HachetteBooks
Instagram.com/HachetteBooks

First Trade Paperback Edition: September 2023

Published by Hachette Books, an imprint of Perseus Books, LLC, a subsidiary of Hachette Book Group, Inc. The Hachette Books name and logo is a trademark of the Hachette Book Group.

The publisher is not responsible for websites (or their content) that are not owned by the publisher.

Print book interior design by Six Red Marbles.

Library of Congress Control Number: 2022940630

ISBNs: 9780306826764 (trade paperback); 9780306826757 (hardcover); 9780306831379 (Signed Edition); 9780306831386 (B&N Black Friday Signed Edition); 9780306831393 (B&N.com Signed Edition); 9780306826771 (ebook)

Printed in the United States of America

LSC-C

Printing 1, 2023

This book is dedicated to anyone who has taken accountability for having behaved like a reprehensible piece of shit and let that inspire them to stop behaving like a reprehensible piece of shit. And to Lux, for accepting me with all of my shitty baggage.

Contents

Introduction

Age Is Way More Than Just a Fucking Number

This book started as a joke. I mean, how could it not? The very idea that I would be writing a book to impart my wisdom to others, that people would be coming to me—a recovering alcoholic drug addict who once willingly tried to cross a pit full of alligators on a tightrope while wearing a jockstrap—for advice about anything is clearly absurd. Surely, if you're looking to Steve-O for help with your life, you are well and truly fucked, right?

Well, maybe.

Let me allow you behind the curtain for a second here: I wrote a book about twelve years ago. Maybe some of you read it. It chronicled my insane, near-suicidal descent into drugs, booze, and, well, near-suicidal insanity, and then my slow crawl back from the edge. When that book came out, I was freshly sober, the third *Jackass* movie had just been a number one box office hit, and I had recently started to tour as a stand-up comedian. So, smooth sailing and happily ever after, right?

Not exactly. For starters, I was only thirty-six years old when that book came out. For a long time, I had thought there was no way I'd live to be even that old. The way I had been going, I don't think many people would've bet on it. Even putting aside all the booze and the drugs, I'd spent most of my teenage and adult years doing incredibly foolish, often quite dangerous stunts, and occasionally getting paid for it. But there I was in my mid-thirties, very much alive, and realizing that if the average life expectancy stats were accurate, I probably wasn't even halfway through my journey. While most people would greet this realization as a profound gift, I guess I'm not most people. I freaked the fuck out.

Getting older has always scared the shit out of me, and I had long figured that I'd avoid having to deal with it by doing the sensible thing and dying young. With that option now seemingly off the table, I was looking at the possibility of having more than half a lifetime ahead of me during which the body I'd relied on for my livelihood would be breaking down, my earnings potential would be dropping precipitously, and the public spotlight that I'd ached for since birth would be gradually receding. Being an old attention whore is *not* a good look. I was overcome with anxiety about what the hell I was going to do with the rest of my life and how I was going to eat.

If you're thinking that this is the point where I tell you that's why I got loaded again, it's not a bad guess, but, fortunately, I didn't. I'm fairly certain that would've killed me, or if it didn't, I would've been better off if it had. But I did do all sorts of other ridiculous, self-destructive shit that made the next decade at least as harrowing as the ones before it. Although I've managed to stay sober, sobriety for me is kind of a moving target. The last ten-plus years have been like a game of addiction Whac-A-Mole: sex, sugar, fame, work, spending, meditation—you name it, I probably have a problem controlling my impulses for it. I've spent large parts of the last decade on some frighteningly irresponsible sexual benders. I've been a maniacally strict vegan who won't shut up about his healthy, ethical food choices *and* the kind of guy who can polish off an entire bag of fun-size Butterfingers in one sitting. I had myself hoisted up onto a Hollywood billboard (and duct-taped to it) to promote my comedy special, scaled a one-hundred-and-fifty-foot construction crane (and got thrown in jail for it) to protest SeaWorld, and climbed nearly nineteen thousand feet up a mountain in Peru (with a bunch of YouTube stars) to prove I wasn't a dick. Yeah, dude, I'm fun.

I know: None of this is making a compelling case for me as America's next great self-help guru. Shit, I can barely help myself, so should I really be dishing out advice to anyone else? My life in sobriety has been about as turbulent a roller-coaster ride as it was before I got clean, but as I started thinking about that roller-coaster ride, I realized that if you looked hard and in the right places, there were enough little nuggets of wisdom to be found to suggest I've actually learned some valuable shit from my lifetime of terrible decisions.

I don't want to overstate the usefulness of this book: It's still, like, ninety percent tales of reckless abandon and (often criminal) stupidity. But that leaves a solid ten percent that might actually help some people in how they think about their lives, about growing older, and about whether or not doing snow angels in flaming rocket fuel on their living room floor is a good idea. (Spoiler alert: It's definitely not.)

I'll give you an example of what I'm talking about. A few years ago, I was in bad shape. Now, if you know anything about me and my history, this will be about the least surprising sentence you'll read in this book. So let me be a little more specific. This was 2013. I'd been sober for about five years by then. I wasn't face-down, lifeless and bloody, on a patch of pavement after drunkenly throwing myself off a balcony to impress some girl. (That was 1995.) I wasn't laid up in a hospital bed after setting myself on fire. (That could've been 1997 or 2017.) I wasn't even in jail. (That could have been so many dates that I won't bother to list them all here.) Yet I was still in very bad shape.

At the particular moment that I want to zoom in on, I was having sex in El Salvador, which—*I know*—doesn't actually sound all that bad. But I'd been engaging in a lot of risky sex that year, for reasons I promise I'll get into later on. There was sex with lots of strangers, some of whom I knew just enough about to know that having sex with them could potentially be very unhealthy. Plus, I was nearly forty at the time. It's one thing to be a twenty-three-year-old dude trying to fuck everything that moves. That's kind of what twenty-three-year-old dudes do. But by this point, I was quickly becoming that sad middle-aged loser who is the last one to realize what a sad middle-aged loser he is becoming. After each of these encounters, I'd feel awful and filled with self-loathing, yet it wouldn't be long before I'd be balls-deep in another one. After a particularly troubling one of these couplings, I knew I had to do something about it. That's when I flew to El Salvador to surf, meditate, read, get my mind right, and most important, *not have sex*. Instead, when I got there, I surfed, meditated, read, and then met a random chick from Canada who was backpacking through Central America.

Which brings us back to me having sex in El Salvador. It wasn't the act itself that was so problematic, or even the partner. It was knowing, even while in the very throes of this one-night stand, that I was in the middle of doing the one thing I'd promised myself I wasn't going to do. It was the recognition that I was out of control. *Again.*

On my way back to California, I was disgusted with myself. Shortly after I got home, I went to a therapist who recommended an intensive outpatient sex addiction program. There, I was told that a period of celibacy—maybe a month or two—can help to rewire your brain to reduce the compulsive desire for sexual release. It's a way to jump-start learning a healthier approach to sex. That sounded exactly like what I needed, so I went all in on celibacy: no sex, no jerking off, no heavy petting, no nothing. If I was even having a wet dream, I'd somehow wake myself up before it actually got wet. *That's* commitment. And then I did this for *431* days. For those doing the math, that's almost fifteen months without shooting a load.

"But why?!?!" I hear some of you shouting at the pages of this book. Well, that's the point I want to make. The reason why is because that's *who I am.* It's the way I'm wired. I take everything too far. I always have. Since I was a kid, my brain told me, "If eating one bowl of Fruity Pebbles is good, eating a whole box will be twenty times better!" In fact, I distinctly remember being pissed off that Fruity Pebbles didn't come in a bigger box. What I've learned about myself is that there's pretty much nothing I go halfway on. I turn just about everything I do into drugs.

Look, did that period of celibacy help me? It did, actually. Did it help any more than it would have if I had only done it for sixty days? I doubt it. I turned what was supposed to be a rehabilitative period of sexual abstinence into an epic stunt. I'd been addicted to sex and now I was addicted to celibacy.

All that was part of me learning—or maybe just reinforcing—a truth about myself: I don't do moderation. That's been a pretty important thing for me to understand as I try to navigate the second half of my life. For anyone to tell me, "Steve, you're getting older, you really need to learn how to stop taking everything to the extreme," is completely unhelpful. My inability to do anything in moderation is a defining feature of who I am. It's like the nose on my face. (Actually, it's more inviolable than my nose, which has been broken and rearranged multiple times.) The point is that you've really got to know yourself and be able to identify what's fucking up your life before you have any chance at unfucking it. And *there's* your nugget of wisdom, dude.

So, yeah, you see what I'm saying—like ninety percent crazy, fucked-up shit from my life, ten percent hard-earned wisdom. That's the mix I'm aiming for in this book, and I'm pretty confident that even if that ten percent is full of terrible advice that no one should really follow, the other ninety percent will be entertaining enough that you won't hold it against me.

*   *   *

I know what you're thinking: *Steve-O, if you wanted to just write another memoir, why even bother with all this self-help shit?* Well, I'll let you in on one more valuable truism that my literary agent, my publisher, and most of my family and friends told me when I made a similar query at the beginning of this process: The world really doesn't need *two* memoirs from Steve-O before he even turns fifty. Also, the idea that one day I might end up on *Good Morning America* talking to Robin Roberts about my secrets to living a good life seemed too funny a prospect not to chase.

You see, what I've realized is that my panic about getting older and trying to figure out what to do with the rest of my life is hardly a unique problem. Many of us are scared shitless about aging. Even if you're nineteen and thinking, *Not me! I'm going to be young forever!* I just want to let you know that it's probably not going to shake out like that. We all must face Father Time eventually, and as many people smarter than me have pointed out, that motherfucker is undefeated. So the sooner you start thinking about this stuff, the better, because it will sneak up on you. I know it did me.

A few years ago, I started traveling around on what I called my "Bucket List" comedy tour. It was kind of a one-man show that mixed stand-up with stories and footage of stunts that I'd wanted to do before I kicked the bucket. I had a line that I used at the opening of the show: "I'm in a really fucked-up situation," I'd say to the audience. "I'm Steve-O in my forties." It always got a good laugh, because everyone understood the truth at the core of it. Growing older is a challenge in the best of circumstances, but when your younger years were spent being famous for doing incredibly reckless things with your body, you are kind of exponentially fucked. Most people fear being washed-up and discarded, but celebrities and athletes face that reality sooner than most everyone else.

In this way, my life is just a turbocharged, extreme case study in a phenomenon that applies to virtually every human on the planet: We're going to get old, our bodies are going to fail us, and we're going to die—and that's if we're *lucky*. Growing older is genuinely a hard kick in the nuts. Is this book really going to solve that problem for you? I doubt it. Could it help? Maybe. Will it at least distract you from your fear that life is ultimately just a meaningless slog toward the blank void of death? That sounds like a worthy goal to me.

Look, this is not going to be your typical self-help book, and it's not meant to be read as a how-to guide. I am not some stupid, entitled celebrity claiming to have life all figured out. Well, I may very well be some stupid, entitled celebrity, but I'm not going to pretend I have all the answers. What I have is a lifetime of insane experiences that I've already packed into what has been only—perhaps—little more than half a life. Maybe there's something to be learned from all the mistakes I've made in my life, and even if there isn't, reading about them is bound to make you feel better about the ones you've made in your own.

So, if at times in these chapters, you're straining to understand the larger point of some wild tale I'm relating—if you're thinking to yourself, *What should I be learning from Steve getting his nose broken by Mike Tyson?*—you can breathe easy knowing that there's probably no larger point and nothing to learn. Sometimes a good story is simply a good story. Anything more than that is just a nice bonus.

1

Don't Be Afraid of Dying.
Be Afraid of Getting Old.

Do you remember "Celebrity Death Pool"? It was that gambling fad where people placed bets on when celebrities would die. I was heavily involved in the whole Celebrity Death Pool craze by virtue of being such a popular pick to kick the bucket. Anyone paying any attention to the way I was living in my twenties and early thirties could see that I was a good bet. I'm sure I cost many grim gamblers a great deal of money by not dying. Sorry, dudes.

Celebrity Death Pool is fairly typical of the level of thought most of us are willing to give to death. No one wants to contemplate the reality of their inevitable demise, so we turn it into a glib joke. Which is fine, except that it doesn't change that reality one bit.

The thing is, death really fucks me up. I've pretty much always been obsessed with it. In fact, my whole career is, in a strange way, an outgrowth of the anxiety I had about dying. I wanted to be sure to leave something behind when I was gone from this planet, so I first started videotaping myself doing skateboard tricks I wasn't all that great at, and then crazy-ass stunts that I was only marginally better at.

With the stunt videos, I was always trying to make it look as if I were cheating death. One of my earliest clips showed me hanging by my bare hands from a railing 120 feet off the ground. At the time, I was drunk off my ass, failing out of college, and unable to hold down any sort of job or really do anything that I wasn't in love with doing. When I think about it now, that stunt feels more like courting death than cheating it. At any rate, I figured I was going to fail at life and be dead a lot sooner than later. I wasn't really viewing my death-defying stunts as the start of a career so much as a message in a bottle to future generations. If I could just do enough crazy shit, those videos would continue to play after I died. Then it would be like I wasn't really dead at all. I knew there was a chance one of those stunts would kill me, but I was willing to bet that they were more likely to make me live forever. It's as if I was taunting death because I was mad at it.

When I was first beginning to get serious about doing stand-up, I had a bit that bombed every time I tried it. I'd get up onstage, look out into the crowd at all the expectant faces, and tell them, "I'm pretty sure God hates us." That usually brought forth a reaction that sounded more like discomfort than laughter, but then I'd try to explain my reasoning. "We're the only living thing on Earth that can comprehend the fact that we're going to die. We have only one instinct, which is to survive, and only one guarantee...that we won't. What the fuck? And as we approach this inevitable ultimate fail, we wilt until we rot. What an awful piece of knowledge to grapple with. I mean, a banana can't look in the mirror and say, 'Oh, fuck. I'm bruising. My days are numbered.' A milk carton can't read its own expiration date and think, 'My career is over! I'm a washed-up has-been!' Nope, God reserved this miserable predicament for humans alone. What a dick."

Okay, so maybe it's no surprise that bit bombed. Audiences—even my audiences—don't usually take that kindly to bad-mouthing their Lord and Savior, particularly when they thought they were just coming out to see me do stupid shit onstage and maybe make fun of my own sexual inadequacies. But I think what really upset people about that bit was the premise. Comedy works when it's grounded in honesty, but maybe that was *too* honest. No one likes to be reminded of their own mortality, especially not on a Saturday night at a comedy club. But for a long time, that sort of summed up my feelings about the human experience: totally unfair.

These days, though, I'm a lot more mellow about it. I mean, of course, having to grow old and die still sucks a bag of dicks, but it doesn't tie me up in existential knots the way it used to. This evolution didn't happen overnight. There was no magic moment or secret formula that suddenly made me totally zen about my future nonexistence. In fact, it remains an ongoing process that I imagine will continue to modulate quite a bit between now and my final fire stunt: cremation.

It's worth mentioning that I'm dead serious about that final fire stunt. I do not want to be buried in the ground, and frankly, I think it's borderline stupid and offensive that we as a culture still do that with our dead. Just like "an eye for an eye" makes the whole world blind, burying people makes the whole world a creepy graveyard. It also renders the land unusable for feeding and housing people. So fuck that. I want to burn.

*   *   *

Early one morning in June 2011, I was lying in bed, sound asleep, when my phone rang. I grabbed my phone, glanced at it, and saw that the call was from this girl who worked at TMZ. This was someone I had met a few weeks before when she introduced herself to me while I was doing a book signing. Now, look, TMZ may very well be morally indefensible trash that is contributing to the downfall of America, but as someone who could be accused of the exact same thing, I fucking love it and always have. So I gave this girl my phone number. Plus, yes, she was very cute.

I answered the phone that morning pretty chipper at the prospect of this hot girl calling me. Then I heard what she was calling about.

"I wanted to see if you could give us a comment on Ryan Dunn's death."

Ooof. Holy fuck.

And that was how I found out that the night before, my friend and *Jackass* castmate had gotten drunk and crashed his Porsche, killing himself and his passenger, an ex–Navy vet named Zach Hartwell who had worked as a production assistant on *Jackass Number Two.* To hear about it, like that, felt like a literal body blow. And, no, for once in my fucking life, I did not have a comment on it, even for my beloved TMZ.

Ryan's death, like many deaths, I suppose, was a shock but not entirely a surprise. Before I got sober, the dynamic of our friendship was much like the dynamic of many of my friendships back then: I annoyed the shit out of him, and he barely tolerated me. I kind of respected the fact that he never even bothered to try to hide how much I got on his nerves. But after I sobered up, our relationship deepened, even though Dunn's drinking never slowed down.

When I first started doing stand-up, most of the *Jackass* crew treated my new pursuit like they treated another of my inexplicable interests, Hacky Sacking: They shit on me for it. It didn't bother me much—that's kind of the vibe between all of us—but it meant the world to me that Dunn stood apart from this by being incredibly supportive. He came to see one of my earliest sets, said he was proud of me afterward, and encouraged me to keep going with it.

Our relationship had changed for the better, but I also think that he was always a little bit puzzled by me. I remember sitting around with Dunn while we were on the set of the third *Jackass* movie. I was a hard-core vegan at that point and was munching on raw broccoli. He just shook his head and laughed.

"Dude, you went from eating crack off dead hookers to raw fucking broccoli?" he said. I hope this doesn't really need to be clarified, but for the record, I've never eaten crack off—or even seen—a dead hooker. That was Dunn's sense of humor, and he was stunned by how much my life had changed. I don't think he ever thought the same thing could happen for him.

The last time I hung out with Dunn was a few months before he died. We were appearing together as contestants on an NBC game show called *Minute to Win It*. Basically, we had a minute to complete each of these ten physical challenges in the hopes of winning a million dollars for charity. These kinds of goofy games and bar tricks were the sort of thing I'd been doing for years, so I figured we'd kill this.

(It's also maybe worth mentioning that I specifically recall petitioning the producers of the show to exclude Dunn and have me on all by myself because I thought I was a big enough star that I didn't need to share billing with anyone else. I know that's an extremely unflattering admission that only makes me look like a total fuckhead, but just so we're clear, the point of this book is not to make me look good.)

When I showed up the morning of the taping, Dunn told me he had to run outside and pound a beer. "Before the show?" I asked. He told me that if he didn't have at least a couple of beers he'd be shaking too much to successfully complete the challenges. I had seen these kinds of withdrawal tremors in members of my own family, and they can be pretty gnarly. I asked him if he thought it might be time to think about sobriety. He shrugged and said, by way of explanation, "I'm just an alcoholic." He said it with such resignation—as if this was his lot in life and there was nothing anyone could do to change that fact. He wasn't sad about it or happy about it. It just was.

I know that kind of resignation very well, because that used to be me. On the previous *Jackass* movie, I remember complaining about how I had terrible heartburn to JP, who has long been *Jackass*'s prop master. JP told me he used to get awful heartburn too until he quit drinking, and then it went away. I looked at him, straight-faced, and nodded: "That's good, but what am *I* going to do?"

We had a good laugh about it, but I wasn't really trying to be funny. That was just my thinking back then. The idea that I could stop drinking was completely off the table, a total nonstarter, regardless of whether it might ease my heartburn or result in any other medical miracles. Nothing JP or anyone else was going to tell me would change that. So I knew better than to try to give Dunn some lecture about changing his life. People can't be pushed into getting sober before they're ready. You're more likely to push them away from it. The best you can hope for is to be a good example of what's possible. But he wasn't ready, and that taping was the last time I saw him alive.

The news of Ryan's accident devastated our immediate and extended *Jackass* family. The consensus among the core cast and crew seemed to be that we should gather together in Pennsylvania, where Dunn died, and get stinking drunk. That felt like an odd way to salute your buddy who just died in a drunk-driving accident, but more to the point, I knew that I couldn't be around that and expect to stay sober, so instead I went to my old rehab in Pasadena and spoke to the clients there, to carry a message of recovery. It was slightly weird for me to be crying about losing my friend in a room full of strangers, but I truly believe it was exactly where I needed to be.

In the days and weeks after Dunn's death, my reaction was perhaps a little surprising: I was jealous. I mean, sure, I was sad. I felt bad for his girlfriend, for his friends, and for his family. I felt bad for *Jackass* and, of course, for myself. But I didn't feel bad for Ryan. In my head, he'd gone out on top. We'd just had the number one movie in the country. He wouldn't have to experience the long, slow fade from relevance, the potential indignity of financial desperation, or the decay of his physical body. He lived fast, was adored by millions, and then he was gone. He got to check out before anyone forgot about him or saw him in any state he may have wished for them to forget. No matter how much spiritual growth I achieve, I think I'm always going to see that as a win.

I guess that's a pretty fucked-up way of thinking. I had defended this position years earlier with *Jackass* director Jeff Tremaine. We were talking about who we would rather be: Flavor Flav or Ol' Dirty Bastard. Two rappers, both troubled, both with issues with drugs and the law, but the former had chugged along, with periodic revivals on reality TV and Public Enemy albums, while the latter had died of a drug overdose at thirty-five. Tremaine was a Flavor Flav guy, but I was all in on ODB. To me, there was no contest: It was better to burn out than to fade away.

I knew very much what the opposite looked like, because I'd seen it, up close, with my own mother. I loved Mom and she understood me in a way no one ever has because we were so much alike. She was an alcoholic and suffered a brain aneurysm before *Jackass* even got started. For five years, she clung on to life, but what she was doing during those years could hardly be considered living. She was heinously disabled, both physically and mentally, was constantly in excruciating pain, needed round-the-clock care, and could barely communicate. Witnessing my mother's suffering for the last five years of her life, hearing her cry, traumatized me far more than anything I've ever been through, and when she finally died, I'm not at all ashamed to say that I was relieved. I gave a blow-by-blow accounting of all that in my first book and I'm not going to relive it this time around, but having seen a person's body fail them so egregiously, to know firsthand how much it is possible for human beings to suffer, imprinted itself on me in a way that I'm still coming to terms with. The inescapable takeaway of Mom's ordeal was that our bodies are going to betray us and it's not going to be pretty.

*   *   *

For most of us, this betrayal is going to be more gradual. I'm happy to report that has been the case with me thus far, but the reckoning that comes with it can still be dramatic.

Not too long ago, I was standing on the fourth rung of a stepladder, looking down into a kiddie pool. At that moment, I was experiencing an emotion that I didn't expect to feel right then: I was really fucking scared. I was practicing for an exceedingly silly stunt that I had cooked up in which I was going to set a new world record for the highest belly flop ever into a kiddie pool filled with urine. Because of course I was. I'd been collecting urine—my own and a few others'—in plastic jugs for months, but for practice, the kiddie pool was filled with water. My plan was eventually to jump from the top of my RV, but I was slowly working up to that height, and at this point, on that ladder, I was less than three feet above the water. So what the fuck was I so scared of?

If you know me at all, you might be aware that jumping from great heights into pools of water is kind of one of my things. When I was a teenager, I'd jump from the roof of our house, over the patio, into our swimming pool. During the time I spent as a homeless vagrant on the campus of the University of Miami (after failing out of classes there and getting kicked out of the dorms), I became friendly with guys on the diving team who I think were at least moderately impressed with my willingness to hurl myself off the diving platforms and attempt various flips and tricks despite having terrible form and no real sense of what I was doing. From there, I graduated to leaping from the tops of three- and four-story apartment complexes into the relatively shallow pools below, jumping from a ten-meter diving platform while wearing stilts, and doing flips off bridges, including one from a trampoline in the back of a moving pickup truck. So, again, why on earth should I be afraid of splashing into a kiddie pool that was only a few feet beneath me?

Well, for starters, because I knew it was going to hurt. Obviously, that's never been a big obstacle for me in the past, but the previous few years had taught me something about my body: It wasn't exactly as resilient as it had once been. When I think of all the crazy stuff I did when I was younger, either with the *Jackass* guys or on my own, it's quite shocking how rarely I got seriously injured. Sure, I landed myself in the hospital doing all sorts of dumb shit—drunkenly throwing myself off a balcony and face-planting on the pavement below, lighting my face on fire while doing a fire-breathing backflip—but all that stuff healed just fine and didn't really do any lasting damage.

But as I've gotten older, the hospital trips have seemed to grow more frequent. In 2016, I shattered my ankle trying to do a skateboarding stunt that involved the legendary skater Danny Way driving a car into a wooden porta-potty I was perched on. That one required surgery, a metal plate, and eleven screws to fix. The following year, I set myself on fire doing snow angels in flaming rocket fuel on my living room floor. The pain from that ordeal takes the prize as the most excruciating I've ever felt in my life, and I needed skin grafts from cadavers to set me right. Filming *Jackass Forever*, I got knocked out cold jumping onto an industrial-strength treadmill carrying a trombone, and then snapped my collarbone trying to hit a ramp on a wakeboard while being pulled by a horse.

It was the second of those wipeouts, on the wakeboard, that was maybe the most concerning. Not because of the injury—although it did mean getting two metal plates screwed into my collarbone—but because my mentality as I was trying to pull it off: I was having a hard time willing my body to do it. Over and over, we'd reset the stunt, and again and again, I'd bail out and let go of the towrope before I hit the ramp. Each time I'd wuss out, I'd get more frustrated with myself. What was it that was making me so hesitant? I'd certainly done crazier shit than this. Why couldn't I just nut up and do it? Finally, I held on just long enough to hit the jump but not long enough to complete it, so I crashed and wrecked my collarbone. Without question, it was my fear and lack of commitment that got me hurt. It's the same feeling I had staring at that kiddie pool.

They say that old people often get injured in falls because they start to distrust their own bodies, and while my wipeouts might not be your typical geriatric spills, I can see the same thing starting to happen with me. It's not just that as you age your body grows more brittle; it's that a part of your brain that you can't shut off starts calculating the physical and emotional costs of getting hurt. On some level, I know I have a lot more to lose these days than I did when I was twenty-five.

There is an emotional fallout that accompanies the physical

one. Maybe the only thing worse than your body failing you is the *knowledge* that your body is failing you. Not being able to be the person you were in your younger years is a serious psychological reckoning. Maybe that's why dudes with receding hairlines start buying high-performance sports cars and dating women twenty-five years younger than they are. They're trying to recapture the ineffable feeling of their youth. It's like a drug.

I'm thrilled to inform you that I did eventually conquer my fear and complete that belly flop off the top of my RV into a kiddie pool of piss. I didn't even get hurt. I've done many stunts that looked more impressive than that one, but I have to tell you, when my face hit that urine, it felt like sweet relief. The feat that I'd pulled off wasn't simply a ten-foot face-plant into a kiddie pool—it was a leap of faith, a victory over my own aging body and mind.

*   *   *

Even in the best of circumstances, aging gracefully is hard. But if you've relied on your body and your youth for your work and your identity, it's a real bitch. It fucks me up to see retired sports stars and UFC fighters dealing with permanent injuries, struggling to make ends meet, even having trouble keeping track of their thoughts because of all the hits they've taken over the years. In fact, it's not just athletes. Seeing footage of once-vital performers like Buster Keaton or Evel Knievel trotting themselves out in their old age, no longer at their physical peak but still in need of both money and public attention, is hard to watch. When I saw *Stan & Ollie*, that movie about the aging Laurel and Hardy, I felt depressed for days.

No doubt, my extreme reaction to this stuff is rooted in the fact that I can see the outlines of my own life in theirs. I mean, part of *Jackass*'s initial appeal was the gleeful stupidity of youth. Just the way we were throwing ourselves around, abusing our bodies, was in itself kind of a celebration of the invincibility you feel when you're young. So what does all that mean now that we're all in our late forties and fifties and still making *Jackass* movies? That's a tough question to answer.

On one level, we've incorporated the "we're too old for this shit" aesthetic into the creative process. It's part of the joke. When Chris Pontius and I did a bit that involved a bunch of us getting naked, holding one another's ankles, and rolling down a hill as "human pinwheels," we introduced the segment by saying, "If you think being middle-aged is a reason to stop getting butt naked and rolling around with your buddies, you're wrong!"

Similarly, I did another stunt that involved me and Machine Gun Kelly racing against each other on these jury-rigged stationary bikes, with the loser getting swatted off the bike by a large mechanical hand. I made the whole thing a chance to prove that in my mid-forties, I could outrace a guy sixteen years younger than me. I was not going to let Father Time win. (And, it should be noted, I did not.)

All that said, is there maybe a point where watching us do all this stupid shit and hurting ourselves becomes less funny and more sad? Certainly. Is it possible that we've hit that point and we don't even know it yet? I don't think so, but I guess it's not for me to say.

This is kind of the elephant in the room with *Jackass* now. I think Johnny Knoxville would say that watching a frail old man try to pull off a stunt and fail is funnier than watching some svelte twenty-five-year-old do the same thing. That may be true, but it's definitely a matter of opinion. As much as I am in awe of Knoxville's dedication, after all the concussions he's had, it pained me to watch him do some of the stuff he did for *Jackass Forever.*

Knoxville has always had a thing for bulls. In *Jackass Number Two*, he did a bit where he stood in front of one blindfolded, smoking a cigarette and wearing a bright red shirt. The bull—who technically was a yak, not that it matters—charged, scooped him up, and flipped him, which was a pretty rad sight and made for an epic clip. He also did something called the Toro Totter, which was basically him, Bam Margera, Ryan Dunn, and Chris Pontius all riding this four-person seesaw trying to evade a bull that was doing its best to gore them. It ended with Knoxville getting stomped pretty hard by this bull. I could barely watch.

For whatever reason—maybe a rare streak of sanity—I don't fuck with bulls at all, so to see Knoxville's willingness to consistently put himself in harm's way with these fifteen-hundred-pound monsters is always horrifying. For *Jackass Forever*, he did another bull bit. In this one, he got scooped up into the air again, but this time he did a flip and a half and landed on his head. He was out cold, snoring. He got stretchered off and ambulanced to the hospital, where they determined he had a broken rib, a broken wrist, and a hemorrhage on his brain. Would it have made any difference if Knoxville had done that stunt when he was younger? Would it have ended any differently? I'd fucking say so, yeah. But regardless, concussions, head trauma—these things pile up over time. The cost-benefit ratio shifts.

Amid this somewhat fragile dynamic, *Jackass Forever* also saw the introduction of a younger generation of cast members: a rapper/actor/stuntman who goes by Jasper Dolphin; a hilarious pro surfer named Sean "Poopies" McInerney; a stand-up comedian named Rachel Wolfson; Eric Manaka, who had starred in the film *Action Point* with Knoxville; and Zach "Zackass" Holmes, who'd had his own MTV show back in 2018. Without a doubt, the mere presence of this new crew pushed us all to up our game, and I'd be lying if I said the old cast didn't feel threatened by them.

There has always been an inherent competitiveness within *Jackass*. Everyone is striving to outdo each other to get the best footage, since only the best footage will make it onto the screen, so it's only natural for any newcomers to be viewed with a bit of jealousy and resentment. I imagine it's not all that different from how someone feels when their new colleague at work is twenty years younger, slimmer, better-looking, and maybe more motivated to prove themselves. Fortunately, in our case, all the new cast members were so happy to be there that it made it pretty hard not to like them immediately. But it did open up the question of what comes next for *Jackass*. Is this the beginning of handing off the franchise to younger performers as the old crew is gently put out to pasture? I mean, if there's yet another *Jackass* movie in ten years, and we're all closing in on sixty, is it still funny to watch us hurt ourselves?

For me, personally, there are really only two possible scenarios I can envision if *Jackass* came around again as I was closing in on sixty. In scenario A, I'm financially secure, I'm in good health, my career is going great, and I'm being offered a chance to spend time doing shit I love, laughing with my buddies and making money. So that's a yes from me. In scenario B, my career has tanked, I'm desperate for cash, I've got a slew of health issues, and I'm being offered a chance to spend time doing shit I love, laughing with my buddies and making money. So that's still a yes from me. Obviously, my motivation would be pretty different in each of those scenarios—I'd rather not be *Stan & Ollie*, leaning on old tricks in a way that's uncomfortable to watch—but the decision wouldn't change. And what's funny is I'm not sure which scenario is more likely to produce better results on-screen.

Knoxville has said that *Jackass Forever* is the end of the line for *Jackass*, and that may very well be the case, but he's declared outright that every one of these movies would be the last, so who knows? A more pressing question for me is, what am I going to do with the rest of my time? I recognized a while ago that, as much as I love doing crazy stunts, my body is not as eager for punishment as it was when I was in my twenties. Part of the benefit of starting to do stand-up, a little more than ten years ago, was that I could go out and make a living without feeling the need to bleed every night.

When I started doing my multimedia Bucket List comedy tour a few years ago, it was a deliberate attempt to blend the anarchic stunts I'd become known for with stand-up comedy in a way that was endurable night after night. The stunts themselves were filmed in advance, then screened at each show. The comedy came in describing the ridiculous stories behind the stunts. It was easily my most successful comedy tour and a nice indication of what could be a sustainable path forward for me. Or as sustainable as any path can be that includes jerking off and blowing a load while falling out of an airplane as one of its core set pieces.

I'm so stoked on the Bucket List show that I'm touring with right now that I am convinced if things fall the right way when I tape a special of it, I could be touring arenas after it comes out. I've also got another show pretty well mapped out that I'm calling Gone Too Far. It will feature a bunch of stunts I'm planning that the people in my life who genuinely care about me have been aggressively trying to talk me out of doing: getting a dick tattoo on my forehead, having a bullet shot through both my cheeks, and getting a boob job, among other ideas. As reckless as these ideas clearly are, it may be even more reckless to put them down in writing as some sort of promise, but I'm so fucking determined to do this shit that I can't imagine a scenario where this stuff doesn't happen.

It's worth mentioning that my fiancée, Lux, really hates the idea of me getting a boob job. In fact, I think she may hate it more than the plan for me to get shot in the face, which probably says something. If I'm being honest, on some level, the boob job is a reaction to the fact that these days when I look in the mirror I can genuinely see the early stages of man-boobs already taking shape on my chest. So why not lean into the indignities of getting older, right? Plus, I can't wait to see the reaction when I flash people.

I'm continuously amazed by the way my friend Tony Hawk is managing his own battle with aging. He's still the most famous skateboarder in the world, and yet he regularly posts videos of himself struggling to do tricks he used to be able to pull off with ease. He recently did a 720, and the caption he included with the video announced that he suspected it was the last one he'd ever do. There is undeniable sadness in such a proclamation, but Tony isn't hiding from any of it; he isn't trying to pretend he's the younger version of himself. He seems to accept that this is all just how life goes, and I respect the hell out of the way he's living it.

*   *   *

Getting old is rarely a very dignified process. If you look at how old people are treated, certainly in America, it's pretty disconcerting. We hide our elderly in nursing homes, in retirement communities, and at all-you-can-eat early-bird buffets, because, frankly, I don't think we want a walking, talking reminder of our own grim future. Forget all the kind words people might have about "the Greatest Generation," forget any ideas of honoring our forbearers—the horrible truth is, old people are widely viewed as a party foul. The way I see it, as a society—at least in most of the Western world—we have collectively decided that we don't want to look at the elderly.

This is the part where I'm going to sound like a Hollywood douchebag as I blather on about how my studies of Eastern spirituality have led me to believe that those cultures have a much healthier view of death. The thing is, though, they really do. As a result, older people command genuine respect in those cultures. The idea of death being simply a part of the life cycle—as opposed to being simply a major bummer—is not only spiritually sound; it's scientifically sound too. If we block out any thoughts of death and refuse to make any preparations for it, of course we're going to be fucking terrified of it. But if we look at the end of life with the same sort of unflinching eye that we look with at the beginning and middle of it, if we watch others go through it, that end becomes demystified and less frightening.

But that's not the world most of us live in right now.

Contemplating our mortality is not popular. We warehouse old people in hospices and nursing homes to avoid having to see it encroaching. This sucks for all sorts of reasons, but it particularly scares the shit out of me. I have referred many times already to the fact that I have a wildly overdeveloped need for attention. I've pretty much been that way since birth, and it has driven me to do most everything I've done in my life. I'm a guy who has regularly set himself on fire in order to get people to look at him. So what's going to happen when I'm old, wrinkly, and gross, and the world is disgusted by the sight of me? What lengths will I need to go to get attention?

These are frightening questions for me to consider, and they have really forced me to reassess my future. If I'm in my sixties, and I still need to be regularly putting my body at risk so the spotlight is trained on me—shit, that will be a tough spot to be in. Of course, it's possible that doing stand-up will provide an elegant solution to this problem, or that I'll find myself some other media job that doesn't require consistent bodily sacrifice. But those aren't exactly outcomes I can bank on, so I need to be ready for a future that doesn't include them.

The uncomfortable truth is the same truth that applies to just about everyone: If your happiness relies primarily on the attention and praise of masses of people you don't even know, you're pretty much fucked. I know that's pretty fucking rich coming from a guy like me, but that doesn't make it untrue. This seems particularly relevant in the social media era, when we're all competing with each other for the likes and smiley-face emojis provided by anonymous strangers. Look, there's nothing wrong with wanting to be liked, with wanting to be noticed, but at a certain point, I know that I've got to learn to be happy with just the attention and love of a much more select group of people: family and friends.

Not too long ago, I was visiting my dad in South Florida. When I'm there, I go to a men's sobriety support group that meets at a train station. It's called...wait for it...Men on Track. Since it's South Florida, the group is filled with tons of old, gray, retired dudes in their seventies and eighties. This group has been going on for a long time. They've been sober together for decades and have developed this insane bond. They're like brothers, ribbing each other, supporting each other when they need it. I find the whole thing so inspiring. I look at the friends I have now—most of them sober buddies—and think, *Shit, getting old may suck, but it's going to suck a hell of a lot less with these guys around.* I tell them that as well, and it means so much to me that they see it the same way I do.

In the last ten years or so, I've also begun to subscribe to the idea that if I'm going to thrive in old age, I need to have a life partner who will stick by me through thick and thin, no matter how thick or thin I get, no matter how shitty I look or feel. I don't think that's the case just for exhibitionist lunatics with fragile egos either. I think the longing to find someone to grow old with is pretty universal. It's a total fucking cliché, but life really is better when you have someone to share it with, or at least someone who will wipe your ass for you when you can no longer reach your butthole. Of course, when I started to come to this conclusion, I was a newly sober narcissist with a raging sex addiction—so, yeah, a total catch. If I was going to turn myself into someone worth spending the rest of your life with, I had a shitload of work to do.

2

Don't Let Fucking Fuck You Up

When I got sober in 2008, I dove into sobriety the way I dive into everything—hard, fast, and with my whole being. After bouncing between psychiatric wards and rehab centers for the first six months, I lived in a halfway house until I'd been clean and sober for a full two years. This wasn't because of some kind of court order. I just understood how shitty the odds are for addicts and alcoholics to maintain long-term sobriety. The statistic I'd heard was that only five percent pull it off, and I knew that I'd need every advantage I could give myself to get into that elite group. I did all the stuff that was suggested to me as a program of recovery, spoke about it whenever anyone pointed a camera in my direction, and basically lived in this bubble community of sober people. It occurs to me that perhaps I was just replacing my addiction to drugs and alcohol with an addiction to sobriety, but I think anyone would agree that was way healthier for me.

A little more than two years into my sobriety, I flew to San

Antonio to go to an international convention for sober alcoholics. They only have these conventions once every five years, and it's a big deal. This was a giant, four-day event at the Alamodome—something like twenty thousand people attended—and at least for those four days, the place had the feel of a spiritual mecca that devotees had made a pilgrimage to reach. I spent my days listening to people share traumatic, inspiring tales of pain and redemption. I spent my nights trying to get laid. Because that's kind of how I rolled at the time.

I remember one night, I met up with a girl from back in L.A. who had come to the convention with a large group of people I knew. She came back to my hotel room with me, and I was doing my best to turn on the charm. She was, at best, only mildly charmed. She made it clear that she didn't want to fool around in any serious way, and after that, it wasn't long before she left.

At that point, I pretty much turned into a werewolf, albeit a werewolf whose only interest is finding someone to suck its dick. I went downstairs to the hotel lobby and immediately zeroed in on a girl who was working behind the bar. Now, I wasn't drinking and I wasn't necessarily tempted to, but just the fact that I was so quick to belly up to a bar while I was in town for a fucking sobriety convention was automatically an awful sign.

As a general rule, it's important for me to check my motivation for being in a place where people are drinking. That doesn't mean I can't ever be in bars. As a guy who has been doing stand-up comedy for more than a decade, I'm regularly surrounded by drunk people, but I have a legitimate reason for that to be the case. Occasionally, there are other legitimate reasons.

But hanging out at a bar to hit on an eighteen-year-old bartender (like a lot of states, you only need to be eighteen to serve alcohol in Texas) probably does not qualify as legit.

Nonetheless, there I was doing my best to convince this girl to hang out with me after her shift was over. She was game but very nervous about being seen fraternizing with a hotel guest, which was strictly forbidden for staff. So she picked me up a few blocks away in her car but then couldn't figure out where to go next. My room at the hotel was off-limits. She told me she still lived at home with her mom, which didn't sound like a particularly romantic setup. You might think the very fact that she was *eighteen years old and still living at home with her mother* would have given me—a then thirty-six-year old man—some pause, but it most certainly did not. We spent a while driving around downtown San Antonio, trying to figure out a place where we could hang out. We sat on a park bench by the River Walk, but it was palpably awkward. Eventually, we decided that the best option was actually to go back to her house, mom and all.

So there I am in this girl's childhood bedroom, half naked, with her stuffed animals looking down on us disapprovingly. We weren't there that long before she got super uncomfortable with the situation and decided to go downstairs and sleep on the couch. At that point, I did the only thing I could: I rolled over and went to sleep in this girl's twin bed. The next morning, I crawled out of bed, went downstairs, and there was her mom cooking breakfast. If that sounds like a whole new level of awkward, it most definitely was, and it only got worse when her mom had to drive me back to the hotel later that morning.

That sort of behavior was pretty much par for the course for me back then. There seemed to be no limit to what I would do for even a chance to have sex.

*   *   *

Life as a touring stand-up comic can be a *Groundhog Day*–like slog in which each day is largely indistinguishable from the one before it. That said, touring was kind of the perfect environment for the steady progression of my sexual addiction. I'd get onstage each night and perform a set filled with stories of wild and ridiculous sex with random groupies, which was a signal to anyone in the audience that I was totally game for wild and ridiculous sex with random groupies, which often led to more promiscuous encounters, which I'd then incorporate into my show.

I can remember once getting back to my hotel room after a show and a meet and greet, emptying out my pockets, and finding a small piece of paper. I opened it up and in girly handwriting it said something like, "I'd love to hang out with you! Call me!" Then it had a phone number. I had no memory of anyone handing me this note, no memory of any woman at the meet and greet cozying up to me, nor did I recall thinking that any of the women there were particularly attractive, but I could think of only one reason why this piece of paper ended up in my pocket and I was very interested in that reason. So I called the number and invited this woman, sight unseen, to my hotel room. It was essentially the equivalent of seeing "For a good time, call…" on a bathroom wall, then thinking, *Yeah, that sounds like a good idea*, and calling the number. I wish I could give you vivid details on what this woman actually looked like or how having sex with this total stranger felt, but I have almost no recollection of it at all. Anonymous hotel room sex with virtual strangers was not an extraordinary event for me in those days.

Another time, after a show in Mississippi, I tried to go back to my hotel room alone, but I didn't make it more than a few minutes before I was feeling antsy. I could sense that solitary reflection on my king-size bed was not going to cure what ailed me. I went downstairs and prowled the lobby of the Hard Rock Hotel and Casino where I was staying, looking for someone who might want to get naked with me for a few hours, but I found no promising candidates. So I returned to my room and shifted to plan B: scrolling through Twitter, hoping to find a DM from a girl in the area who wanted to "hang out." Lo and behold, there was one, but she didn't have a profile picture on her Twitter account, just that little egg that Twitter used to put there as a placeholder for people who didn't upload photos. No matter—I invited her to come to my hotel room anyway. As soon as I did, I regretted it. *I have no idea who the hell this person is. What the fuck was I thinking?* When there was a knock on my door thirty minutes later, my first instinct was to be silent and hide underneath the bed. But my curiosity outweighed that first instinct, so I crept quietly to the hotel room door and peaked through the peep hole. As it turned out, she wasn't bad-looking. I invited her in.

We got to talking—because even in these kinds of situations, I was nothing if not a gentleman—and I asked her what she did. She didn't mince words: "I'm a webcam whore." She actually said that, then proceeded to tell me some stories about life as a webcam whore, which, it turns out, is about as fucked-up as the job title suggests. In among these torrid tales, she mentioned that her breasts were horribly scarred from a botched boob job. She told me that guys often turned very mean when she took off her top. Duly warned, you might think that this would be the point where I finally pulled my shit together and politely bid this nice woman a fond adieu. But if you think that, you really haven't been paying attention. Remember, I'm a gentleman. I wasn't about to let this woman leave my room feeling unloved. I generously allowed her to give me a blowjob. Because that's the kind of guy I am.

I'd be lying if I said I didn't have a whole lot of fun acting out sexually, but just like with booze and drugs, in sexual addiction, the highs get harder to achieve and maintain and the lows get deeper and more sustained. The desperate and never-ending chase grows increasingly sad and pathetic. I think I was trying to use sex to build my self-esteem. You see, if a woman was willing to fuck me, that seemed to excite the same set of neurons in my brain as having a bunch of people gasp at one of my stunts or laugh at my jokes. I can't promise that the neuroscience behind that theory totally checks out, but it makes plenty of sense to me.

It wasn't just a parade of forgettable one-night stands. If it was, I might not have felt as awful about it as I eventually did. With a one-night stand, especially someone I might meet on tour, there is a pretty good understanding from both parties as to what is going on. Most people don't get too emotionally invested in it.

But I also developed a pattern of behavior that went much further. I hurt people on a deeper level, and closed myself off from the possibility of building a fulfilling, long-term relationship with anybody. My M.O. was pretty much the same every time: I'd meet some woman, get way into her, pour on the charm to convince her I really cared about her (which I invariably thought I did), sleep with her a few times, then quickly lose interest and ghost. Wash, rinse, repeat. I'd feel increasingly terrible about acting like this, about being so utterly reckless with other people's feelings, but I was powerless to keep myself from doing it again and again. It was as if in the early stages of this cycle, I'd be so enamored with these women that I'd be sure that *this time would be different*, even though a part of my brain—the smart part—had to know that of course it wouldn't be.

I have no doubt that is a familiar pattern of behavior for lots of people, whether you consider yourself a sex addict or not. You don't need to have any fame or money to be a sleazy asshole. This became such a pattern for me that my friends and I even coined a term for a particular subset of these encounters. When I'd take an interest in a woman who didn't live in L.A., part of my hard-core charm offensive would be to offer to fly her into town and show her around. This was called "the import program." We'd go for a hike, we'd get a photo together in front of the Hollywood sign, we'd go to the beach and I'd make sure she got a photo of herself standing on a big, soft-top surfboard, riding it in the whitewash. And, of course, for the big highlight of the whirlwind tour, she'd get to have sex with me, a real, live celebrity. (Though, to be frank, the Hollywood sign might have been a bigger highlight for many of those women.) The beauty of the import program was that my fading interest usually coincided neatly with her return flight home.

* * *

The year 2013 was a dark one for me. I had been hosting a show on truTV called *Killer Karaoke*. I'm sure you never saw it, which is fine, because it was a pretty awful show, and I'm not just saying that because I'd been fired from it earlier that year. I'll get more deeply into all that later, but for the time being, all you need to know is that after I got fired, I started trying to drum up a new TV gig and pitched around an idea for a show, which was met with unanimous rejection. That stung. I still had my comedy tour but no assurance that that career path would survive its infancy. With no other jobs looming on the horizon, I was beginning to feel like I had arrived at the beginning of the end of my career. It seemed like I was just banging my head against a wall. This was compounded by the fact that *Jackass* head honchos Johnny Knoxville, Jeff Tremaine, and Spike Jonze were busy that year making *Jackass Presents: Bad Grandpa*. It was a scripted feature film built on hidden-camera footage and pranks that was being done under the *Jackass* banner but without any involvement from the *Jackass* cast except for Knoxville. To me, it felt like he was a lead singer ditching his band to go solo. It was like Michael Jackson leaving the Jackson 5, which, in this case, made me Tito.

To be clear, Knoxville and those guys had done nothing wrong. They had every right to make this movie, and I don't think it was intended as a shot at the rest of the *Jackass* cast. But even if I understood that, it still felt like a gut punch while it was happening and only added to my growing sense that I was washed-up. For a guy like me, who has an innate, desperate need to be the center of attention, feeling like the cameras weren't on me anymore—and, worse, that they might never be again—was a devastating blow to my self-worth. I know it's pathetic, but that's me.

I filled this void in my soul with the one thing that seemed to offer me any relief: sex. I was touring relatively consistently that year, which was helpful in that it put me regularly into the proximity of women who were willing to play their part in my morale-boosting regimen. I went on a real bender. At one point, I was doing shows with Tom Green in Las Vegas when I met this incredibly beautiful woman who was at the show with her boyfriend. I was so laser-focused on getting what I needed that I didn't much care about the boyfriend's presence and hit on her right in front of him. We ended up awkwardly exchanging numbers while he watched, but we never met up that weekend. We did keep in touch, though, and a few weeks later she told me she'd broken up with her boyfriend, so I flew her in to see me.

I was prepared to give her the regular import program routine, but as soon as I picked her up at the airport, I knew all was not well. She was disturbingly rail thin, with her eyes a bit sunken back in her head. I soon discovered she was bulimic and had been doing a lot of purging in the weeks since I'd seen her in Vegas, at least partly because of the anxiety she had about coming to see me. That didn't feel too good. I don't think she had a substance abuse problem, but she seemed troubled and extremely unhealthy.

Nonetheless, we went back to my apartment and almost immediately started having unprotected sex. This wasn't normal operating procedure for me—even in the throes of sexual addiction, I was almost always smart enough to wear a condom—but for whatever reason, in that moment, that's what happened, and that's what continued to happen for the five days she was in town.

Although I was taking her through the usual whistle-stops on the tour—Hollywood sign, surfing, and so on—the whole thing had a very dark tinge to it. Without fail, she disappeared to the bathroom immediately after she finished eating, and admitted to purging all her meals when I confronted her about it. I talked to her a lot about the possibility of 12-step programs as a treatment for her bulimia and urged her not to go on living like this. It's probably a sign of just how dark things were that I was spending that very long weekend trying to somehow "save" this girl while not even recognizing that I was drowning myself.

Toward the end of her visit, when we were hiking, she mentioned to me that the guy she had been with in Vegas, her old boyfriend, was bisexual, and that the person he'd been with before her had been a guy. She mentioned it in passing, as if it was just an interesting little trifle of information, but my brain immediately started overloading with anxiety. All I could think about was that I had spent the last three and a half days having sex with this woman without a condom, and her last boyfriend was in the highest risk category for HIV. I got quiet as I rolled this fact over and over in my mind.

When we got back to my apartment, I told her I had to walk my dogs. As I leashed them up and took them out onto the sidewalk, I whipped out my phone and started frantically Googling statistics about gay men and AIDS, growing increasingly terrified with each new search result. I returned to the apartment in a blind panic. But here's the really insane part: You want to know what I did once I got back there? That's right, I had sex with her again. No rubber.

On one level, my justification was *Hey, no point in putting on an oven mitt after you've already burned your hand on the stove.* But on another level, it was like, *WHAT THE FUCK ARE YOU DOING, YOU FUCKING IDIOT?!?!* I mean, as I was pumping away, I can genuinely remember thinking, *What is wrong with me? What am I doing?* It was then I realized that I really had a problem and needed to do something about it. I figured I had hit rock bottom with my sexual addiction.

As soon as I dropped that girl off at the airport, I raced to the doctor's office to get every possible test for STDs, emphasizing HIV as my main concern. Fortunately, they were all negative. I also reached out to someone I knew who was in a program for sex addiction, asking for help. He brought me to his recovery group, where they gave me some literature to get me started in the program, and I felt totally ready to commit to it.

Turned out, though, what I thought was rock bottom wasn't quite it. I had a bit further to sink. This was the point that I mentioned in the introduction, when I decided to fly off to El Salvador to surf, meditate, and be alone. Instead, I had this surf guide take me into town, where I met a random Canadian chick, and, well, you don't need any more gory details of my adventures in sad-fucking.

When I flew home, I was in a dark place. I began to realize how fucked up my entire attitude toward sex was and had always been. I'd grown up believing in the conquistador approach to pussy. The goal was to "crush as much beav" as humanly possible. If you were cringing as you read that last sentence, it's nothing compared to how much I was cringing when I wrote it. But if I'm honest with myself, that's the guy I was.

It's hard to overstate how ashamed I am about all this. This whole chapter is agonizing to recount because it's painful for me to admit the guy I used to be. I can't easily dismiss this stuff as youthful folly. I was nearly forty fucking years old by the time I started to wake up to all this. For a while, I beat myself up about it—about the damage I caused to other people, about the dick-head I was, about the bullshit things in life that I thought were important. But self-loathing and self-pity are some dangerous emotions, particularly if you've previously used massive amounts of cocaine, ketamine, booze, and nitrous oxide to numb yourself to them.

It had occurred to me before then that my sexual habits were a problem. I'd even been to a couple of support groups in the previous few years, but up until that point, I hadn't been willing to do much to deal with the problem. Now I knew I had to. I was a bad joke, an aging pussy hound. I was being wildly reckless—with my health, with other people's health, and with their feelings. I truly believed that to have any real quality of life in the future, I needed to learn how to be in a healthy relationship. But even if I were to have met the perfect woman at that point, I'd have been completely useless to her. What woman would want to be with a guy who stuck his dick into every warm hole he could find?

I started seeing a therapist who specialized in sex addiction. In one of our first sessions, he asked me if I could commit to sexual abstinence on my next string of stand-up dates. We weren't talking about an extensive stretch, really just a long weekend. Nonetheless, I didn't think I could pull it off. I told him that it was going to be particularly hard because there would be more opportunity than ever: I had sold out more shows in advance than I'd ever done before. He brought up my abstinence from drugs and alcohol, and pointed out that surely there was an abundance of opportunities to get loaded. Why should this be any different? I had no answer to that question, but when he asked it, I could finally see that I was in the grips of an addiction in much the same way I had been before. I wish I could say that realization sorted me out, but still, I couldn't help myself. When I got out on the road for those stand-up gigs, I failed once again to keep my dick in my pants. All the genuine effort I was putting toward this made the shame of my failure feel even worse.

Nonetheless, the therapist continued to preach the virtues of a period of sexual abstinence. He explained that this self-imposed celibacy can often help rewire your brain to think about sex in a healthier way. So, for example, if you have always used sex or jerking off as a way to alleviate stress, every time you do—although it might bring you temporary relief—it's also building up the need to act out like that again and again. It's akin to throwing another log on the fire of your sexual addiction. If you can go for a nice stretch without ejaculating at all, that's supposed to reduce the impulse. He suggested I commit to going two weeks without any sex or masturbating, which seems like an eminently achievable goal for anyone. Well, almost anyone. Despite my solemn vow, after four days, I was in the bathtub alone, and the line between personal hygiene and, uh, romance got a little blurry. The next thing you know, I'd blown it, and my half week of progress was literally down the drain.

After repeatedly showing back up to my therapist's office

with my tail between my legs to admit I had failed once again to adhere to any of his helpful suggestions, he recommended that I go into an intensive outpatient program. In other words, sex addict rehab. My powerlessness to control myself was so self-evident by this point that I quickly agreed to it.

The outpatient program ran from nine a.m. to five p.m. every weekday for two weeks. Although I was well-versed in the language of addiction and recovery, dealing with sex addiction is very different from treating a problem with booze or drugs. With booze and drugs, the goal is simple and measurable: Do not drink, do not take drugs. With sex addiction, it's much more nuanced. The goal is not to eliminate sex from your life, but rather to keep it from controlling your life, causing chaos, and putting you and others at risk. It's all about learning a healthier approach to sexuality.

There were only three of us in the program, and suffice to say that the other two guys made me feel like a pot smoker in a hardcore drug rehab. Still, all three of us took everything super seriously. The days were long, consisting of childhood trauma work and deeply vulnerable group therapy.

After completing this two-week program came the really difficult part: going back out into the world and living it. I started to learn strategies that helped other sober sex addicts maintain their sobriety. An important one is categorizing your behaviors into what we called red-light, yellow-light, and green-light behaviors. It works exactly as you would assume if you've ever seen a traffic light: Green-light behaviors are things that are fine, yellow light means proceed with caution, and red light is not just something that you need to stop doing—it constitutes a relapse. The tricky part is that for each person, what constitutes red-, yellow-, and green-light behaviors is different. For some people, watching hard-core porn is a definite red light. For others, it's a regular old Thursday night. It helps to work with therapists and other people in your support group to figure out where your own lines in the sand are, but more than anything, you have to be brutally honest with yourself. I also learned about the importance of setting up a dating plan, which was essentially a playbook for getting to know a potential partner and beginning a relationship in a healthy way.

The idea of a celibacy period was raised again when I was in the outpatient program, and this time I committed to it with the same fervor I do everything else. I decided that if I was going to be not having sex, I was going to be not having sex harder and better than anyone else ever had. So I quit it all: fucking, jerking off, porn, any sort of even vaguely romantic contact with women. There was no grinding, no making out, and even a long hug had to be viewed with a little suspicion.

At the time, I was touring, so I'd get up onstage every night and treat the audience as if it were a support group. I'd say something like, "It's be forty-nine days since I acted out sexually." Then I'd proceed to tell wildly explicit stories about my previous sexual escapades or some comical early failures at abstinence, which was, in effect, chumming the waters. Women in the audience who might have been vaguely interested in hooking up with me seemed to take this as both an invitation and a challenge to break my celibacy streak.

It wasn't easy—and there were opportunities with drop-dead gorgeous women that I passed up that still pain me a bit to recall. But the harder it got for me to maintain celibacy, the more I was emotionally invested in this streak. It legit made me feel good about myself. I was becoming a better man. As it went on, though, the streak started to take on the qualities of any other epic stunt. As I went six months, nine months, a year without shooting a load, I think what I was really engaged in was sexual anorexia—exhibiting a grotesque form of control over a part of my life that had previously felt distinctly out of control.

As much as I treasured my celibacy streak, it made me an irritable son of a bitch. I was quick to snap at people. If I saw someone filming me with their phone while I was doing a stand-up set, I would just start yelling like a crazy person, "GET THE FUCK OUT!!!" I don't care what Buddhist monks might say, man is simply not meant to go that long without sexual release. But the more I suffered, the more the streak meant to me. I was so hardcore about it that if I was even having a wet dream, the whole idea of my sexual sobriety would enter my dream and I'd somehow wake myself up before I shot my load. It used to piss me off: I wouldn't have considered such a nocturnal emission to be breaking the streak, but I guess some part of my subconscious did.

In the end, the no-jizz life lasted 431 days, which is bonkers. Pretty much every guy whom I've told about this wants to know the same thing: How did it feel when you finally shot your first load in nearly fifteen months? I am disappointed to report that it felt like nothing special. I mean, it was fine, but I think I had been expecting something completely mind-blowing and what I ended up with was just a garden-variety orgasm.

Despite all that, I don't regret the celibacy streak. I mean, for sure, it was unnecessary to carry on for as long as I did, but in the end, it did succeed in changing the way I thought about sex. I think what made me so determined to keep it going wasn't just proving to myself that I could, but demonstrating it preemptively for the woman I knew I hadn't met yet. My mantra was that I was "working to become the man whom the love of my life deserves." The fact that I hadn't yet met the love of my life was the whole point: I had to make myself into someone who would be worthy of that kind of relationship.

In a strange way, I also think those 431 days were some sort of personal penance that I felt a need to perform in order to make up for what an embarrassing Neanderthal I had been for so many years. But in time, and with lots of therapy, what I realized is that being embarrassed about that guy I used to be, cringing at the things I used to say and do, is actually a *good* thing. It means I'm not that guy anymore. I know enough now to be embarrassed.

I'm not the only person in the world carrying around a sexual past that he's not proud of. So many of us lug that baggage from relationship to relationship, never sure of exactly when the right time to unpack it is and, even then, how much to unpack. For me, my sexual addiction and the things I did in service of it have impacted the relationships I've had since I started to treat it. In some cases, it played a part in undoing those relationships.

The one thing I can say, though, is that if someone wants to be with me—the real me—that past, as embarrassing as it often is, is part of the package. I can't hide it or not talk about it and hope that makes it go away. What I've found is that being honest about my sexual history might not fix every relationship or make every woman I spill that history to feel better about who I was back then. But practicing rigorous honesty and holding myself accountable is the only way I'm going to have a chance at not becoming that asshole again.

3

Find Someone Who Will Be with You When the Shit Hits the Fan

Back when I was still loaded on drugs, I had plenty of girlfriends, and most of them were beautiful, intelligent, and thoughtful. But I was a fucking disaster and treated them like shit. I valued cocaine, nitrous oxide, ketamine, PCP, and booze more than I valued other people, which pretty much torpedoed any chance of those partnerships lasting very long.

Once I got sober, so many things in my life changed, but not that. Even without all the recreational pharmaceuticals, I sucked at relationships. Sure, some of it was down to a lot of that shit I wrote about in Chapter 2: It's challenging to be in a fruitful, committed relationship when you're a raging sex addict. But, hey, lots of people struggle in relationships, not just those who derive their self-worth from empty sexual encounters with virtual strangers in anonymous hotel rooms.

Many of us tend to look for a significant other in much the same way we look for a pair of shoes: try some on and see which fit the best. But now imagine you've got to find one pair of shoes to wear for the rest of your life. You're going to want to do more than just walk around the store in them and see how they look in the mirror. You're going to want shoes that look good, that feel great, and that you know will hold up well, even in terrible weather.

In my own life, I have often put only slightly more thought into the women I dated than the shoes I wore. Sometimes I cared only if I thought they looked good in the mirror, or, perhaps more important, if everyone else thought they looked good. (Okay, I'll quit the shoe analogy now. I promise.)

Around the end of 2011, a friend of mine told me that she had a friend named Elisabetta who wanted to meet me. Elisabetta was an Italian supermodel who until recently had been dating George Clooney. What you're thinking right now is what I was thinking back then: Why would an Italian supermodel who had dated George Clooney ever be interested in me? I didn't know, but I was certainly game to find out.

All three of us went to lunch one day, and when I saw Elisabetta in person, I thought for sure someone was fucking with me. Did Knoxville and Tremaine set this up as some sort of elaborate prank to humiliate me? But as we sat there, it became clear this was no prank. As baffling as it was, Elisabetta seemed to actually be into me. We got along well and traded phone numbers.

A few days later, I picked her up in my shitty Nissan Versa and we went to dinner. When I drove her back to her place afterward, she asked me if I wanted to come inside and meet her dogs. I thought long and hard and just about made it until the words had finished coming out of her mouth before I replied, as casually as I could, "Yeah, that sounds cool." We went upstairs to her luxury penthouse apartment in Beverly Hills, and from the minute I walked in, I basically never left. I spent the night and then pretty much moved in to her place for the duration of our relationship.

I know to normal, deliberative humans, this all may seem like things were moving very fast, but as I've mentioned before, when I'm all in, I'm *all* in. I am impulsive by nature, and at that moment, I couldn't think of anything in the world that would make me happier—or perhaps, more important, make me look cooler—than to be around Elisabetta all the time.

The tabloids and the internet reveled in the fact that this ridiculously hot chick had gone from George Clooney to me, and, of course, I reveled in the fact that they were paying so much attention to me. Elisabetta was genuinely kind and caring, on top of being gorgeous, but it's tough to say whether I was more in love with her or with the fact that the whole world couldn't believe I had landed her. It often felt like I was really in a relationship with the attention I was getting for being with her.

It was clear that we weren't a perfect match. After we'd been together for a couple months, I had some tour dates in Florida, so Elisabetta came with me to meet my family. We went to dinner one night with my sister, Cindy, and Elisabetta ordered a chicken entrée and a glass of wine, then stepped outside to smoke a cigarette. At that point in time, I was not only sober and had quit smoking cigarettes, but I was also a publicly militant vegan and animal rights advocate. As soon as Elisabetta got up from the table, Cindy, who has long been the level-headed angel on my shoulder, looked at me, shook her head, and asked, "Steve, what the hell is going on?"

I shrugged and smiled a little sheepishly. "What do you want from me?" I protested to Cindy. "*Maxim* rated her as the seventh-hottest woman in the world!"

You might not be surprised to learn that this is not necessarily the foundation of a long, successful union. Even if it was, I was destined to blow it anyway. Though I didn't always recognize it at the time, I was a selfish dick throughout the relationship, about things big and small. I was constantly insisting that we eat at vegan restaurants even though Elisabetta was not at all a vegan. In fact, she had a hard-core aversion to eating vegetables. Practically the only thing she ever ate was meat, and I didn't consider for one moment that she might like to go to dinner somewhere that actually serves it.

Ultimately, Elisabetta and I were very different people with very different lifestyles. After several arguments that made this abundantly clear, we called it quits.

*   *   *

In 2015, I was offered a spot on this British winter sports reality show called *The Jump*. Appearing as a contestant on a reality competition show wasn't the type of TV gig I had been hoping for—in fact, I considered it a bad look—but the fact that this would only air on British television and promised a six-figure payday to essentially go on a six-week vacation at a ski resort in Austria sounded like a pretty good deal. I said yes.

The show was actually a lot of fun. I had a blast learning shit like ski jumping and skeleton racing, but the reason I'm bringing it up here is because I met another contestant there named Stacey Solomon. She's a British singer and a television host, and she and I hit it off. Now—and this is an important part—at the time we met I was deep into my celibacy run and working hard to deal with my sexual addiction. Back in L.A., I had a therapist, a separate men's therapy group, and a whole support system that was keeping me on track with my sexual sobriety. When I got to Austria, although I did find a 12-step group for drugs and alcohol, I pretty much unplugged from the rest of my support system. Which, in retrospect, explains some of the crazy-ass decisions I made in Austria.

Let's be clear: When I describe my decision-making from that period as "crazy-ass," I'm not talking about my usual sort of crazy. I didn't get loaded again, I didn't set my hair on fire before doing a luge run, I didn't ski off a one-hundred-foot cliff because I thought it would look cool on camera. All those things would've been well within the normal sphere of my lunacy. In fact, they would've been par for the course.

This crazy was all about the way I was with Stacey. When I met her, I could see that she was sweet and smart and funny. There was a definite connection between us, but she resisted getting involved with me, and for very good reasons: She had two young kids and lived in London. I lived in L.A. and was not exactly a good bet. She didn't want to have a meaningless fling, and what future could there really be for us beyond that? Her reasoning was all very sensible.

Mine was not. I became infatuated with her. I was convinced that I needed her to make me whole. I tried to pour on the charm.

This was classic love addiction behavior, something I'd been very prone to in the past and which I'd been trying to set boundaries around in my therapy and support groups. Remember when I told you about red-light and yellow-light behaviors and dating plans? For someone like me, that stuff is important for setting healthy boundaries around really practical parts of getting into a relationship. How often can I text someone I've just met? How often can I go on a date? If I go on a date, can I see the person the next day? I had set up a dating plan to keep from love-bombing someone. Well, with Stacey, I blew through all those red and yellow lights and basically set fire to the dating plan.

Amid all this, I cashed in my celibacy streak at 431 days. There was nothing particularly special about that number. I told myself that the streak was unhealthy—which maybe it was by that point—but ultimately I was just trying to justify a forthcoming run of bad decisions. So, one night in Austria, alone in my room, I cranked one out. As I mentioned before, I had imagined it was going to be a firehose blast of splooge, but in fact it was just a regular old squirt that landed unceremoniously on my stomach. I took a photo of it, though, which I then texted to my men's support group back in L.A., which included the female therapist who leads the group. I'm not sure what reaction I expected out of them, but they were totally fucking appalled. As they should have been. It's worth noting that that was pretty much my only communication with the group the whole time I was in Austria. I never bothered to seek any advice about my pursuit of Stacey.

Stacey, for her part, put up a good fight. When I would declare my deep feelings for her—which I did often—she'd politely balk.

She'd point out all the reasons why it wouldn't work between us. But her reluctance only increased the intensity of my pursuit. Finally, on our last night in Austria, she gave in. Not all the way in, but far enough that the barrier between us was broken.

I was set to fly back to L.A. the next day but had a layover in London, so I rebooked that second leg of my flight and spent several days with Stacey. And then it was really *on*. For the next six months, I spent a lot of time at her home in London. Because she had kids, she couldn't very easily come see me in L.A., so I essentially put the rest of my life on hold and just kind of hung out with her and her kids.

Stacey's career was going great—she had books, a clothing line, voice-over and hosting gigs, music—while I had largely quit working so I could be with her. That part made me very uncomfortable. For a guy who was filled with anxiety about the state of his career, giving up the pursuit of work like that stressed me out. It was as if my compulsion to work, to make money, was running head on into my compulsion to pour myself whole hog into a relationship. It was a kind of death match between my addictions.

Then came the reckoning. Although I resisted seeing it this way at the time, what had happened with Stacey was only a turbocharged version of what had happened with so many of my relationships before her. I was smitten, I lavished her with attention, I got what I wanted, and then I broke it off. I did stick around for six months this time, but that almost made it worse. I had become not only a real part of her life; I'd become a part of her kids' lives too. And then—poof!—I was just gone.

Some people have pointed out to me that Stacey was the one

with the kids, that she ultimately made the decision to bring me into their lives, that it is not necessarily permanently scarring for kids of a single mother to meet a boyfriend and then have him disappear from their lives. But if I'm being honest, none of that makes me feel much better about how I handled that. I had set up plans and boundaries to keep this exact thing from happening, and then I ignored them all. In doing so, I completely disregarded other people's feelings in order to indulge my own.

To this day, I still beat myself up about the way it went down. Ironically, I don't think Stacey does. We aren't really in touch anymore, but she has corresponded with my family and seems to bear no ill will toward me. I take that not as an exoneration of my actions, but more an indication of her own emotional fortitude. If you've ever heard the phrase "hurt people hurt people," you should know that the opposite is also true: Healthy people usually don't. She seems to be a happy, healthy person who can go through life without gigantic grudges and resentments, even when they might be totally justified. What a freak.

*   *   *

After crashing and burning with Stacey, I got myself back on track with my therapy and support groups, and I also tried to learn from my mistakes. For as great a person as Stacey is, not much else about that relationship made any sense. Her life was in London. Mine was in L.A. As much as we all want to believe in the power of love to overcome all obstacles or whatever, being with her, logistically speaking, was always going to involve a lot of compromises, and I've never really been good with compromise.

On the surface, my next relationship made a bit more sense.

I had known Kat Von D a long time, and we had been together years earlier, when I was still very much a drunken, wasted mess of a human. Kat is a world-famous tattoo artist who has starred on multiple reality shows and is an all-around cool chick. The first time around, she had the misfortune of hooking up with me when I was near my worst, and she bore the ugly brunt of my booze and drug regimen as much as just about anyone. Over and over back then I promised her I'd stop taking drugs or that I'd cut back on my drinking or whatever, and there was not one of those promises that I kept. Not even close. When she eventually got fed up and dumped me, I lashed out at her and amplified some hateful nonsense that was going around on the internet about her, even though I knew it wasn't true. Frankly, I was carrying around a lot of shame over the way I'd acted during that relationship and especially after it ended.

It's a testament to her that she never held my behavior against me. In fact, back in 2008, after I had gone completely nuts and was locked up in the psych ward at Las Encinas Hospital in Pasadena, I wrote Kat a letter explaining how much I hated myself for the way I had treated her. She got back to me to say that she didn't feel like my behavior had anything to do with her—it had everything to do with me and what I was going through. I thought that was a highly evolved interpretation of what had been an excruciatingly personal betrayal of her on my part.

Nonetheless, I still found it perplexing that she was willing to have anything to do with me ever again. In the years after I got sober, we'd occasionally run into each other, and she was always friendly. She invited me to an event or two, and at one point she gave me a tattoo. Knowing our history together, her kindness felt wholly undeserved.

By late 2015, we were spending more time together, and our relationship began to take a turn in a romantic direction. In some ways, that felt really healing to me. I had all this gnarly scar tissue from the past, from before I got sober, all this shame for how I'd acted back then, and my reconciliation with Kat made me feel like I had worked past that.

There were a lot of reasons for me to be optimistic about a relationship with Kat. We had so much in common: similar public profiles, both clean and sober, both very into tattoos and heavily into animal rights. Kat was a vegan, and although I wasn't strictly a vegan at that point—I was eating fish and eggs—we had a similar mindset about all that stuff. So, all good, right?

Eh, maybe not. For as much as this match made sense on paper, in real life, we were kind of a nightmare. We argued all the time. It seemed like we couldn't go more than a few days without some sort of conflict bubbling up between us. To be fair, the problem was mostly me being consistently selfish and self-centered. I expected the relationship to revolve around me and my needs, and when it didn't, I'd often have a tantrum.

I was a lot to handle. I was a sex addict who seemed to love nothing more than talking about being a sex addict. Like everything else in my life, I felt happy to share my ongoing struggles with whomever was around me, and I wasn't bothered if they had a microphone or a video camera with them. Kat wasn't okay with that. For someone who has lived so much of her adult life in public, she's an intensely guarded person. She was very sensitive about her privacy. She didn't want me talking about my sex addiction, and she wasn't really cool with me sharing the intimate details of our life together with a room full of men at a group therapy meeting.

She also didn't like me getting onstage at comedy clubs and talking about my sexual history. In fact, within about a week or two of us getting back together, I was scheduled to tape my first comedy special. I was recording two shows back to back, and the special would comprise the best material from those shows. Now, Kat had seen my act prior to this. She knew that I talked about sex in graphic and embarrassing ways onstage. But she had never sat in the audience and watched all this while we were in a relationship together. And now she was going to.

So I get up onstage and do my usual bits. I tell a story about getting a blowjob from a girl with no teeth. I tell one about a four-way with three women in an Austin hotel, and another about going down on a stripper. I regale the audience with a tale about having anal sex with a girl who, uh, had not cleared the chamber, so to speak, before the encounter. As you can imagine, it's all very classy and tastefully rendered.

Well, after that first show, I go to find Kat, and she's nowhere. Not backstage, not in her seat, not in the lobby, not on the curb outside. It turned out, she'd gone back to the hotel. She simply couldn't bear to watch anymore. Needless to say, when I got back to the hotel after the second show, things were not okay between us. The fact that the comedy special was set to air on Showtime a few months later proved to be a ticking time bomb for our relationship. She was mortified at the idea that all this shit would soon be widely available.

I should note that these were not unreasonable feelings on her part, but they were so antithetical to the way I've always operated. I want the world to look at me all the time, for whatever reason, good or bad. Kat isn't like that. She's private. She views celebrity culture and the media ecosystem around it with grave suspicion. I view it as vital to keeping me alive and well fed. The fact that I got most of my news from TMZ was a problem for Kat. That I was a devoted listener of Howard Stern was an even bigger problem. I'd reach out to TMZ to seek publicity. I'd call in to Stern to tell on myself for whatever stupid shit I'd done recently. Kat couldn't conceive of doing such things. That was like being in bed with the enemy to her. This kind of stuff would drive her nuts.

I have no doubt that Kat's approach to all this is way healthier than mine. But this wasn't something where I could just convince myself of the rationality of her approach and then adopt it myself. Rationality plays no part in it for me. I am an attention whore deep in my soul, and that wasn't something I could just wash away with reason. And this created a pretty fundamental difference between us.

That whole relationship was hard. I think we argued so much because we genuinely cared about each other and wanted it to work out. But we just kept ramming our heads up against these same brick walls over and over. In the end, when it fell apart less than six months after it started, it was painful. We didn't part on particularly good terms. We're not friends now. She blocked me on her social media and scrubbed any trace of me from her life. I get it.

It's ironic, I guess, that after I'd been such a fucking asshole during our first go-round, Kat was able to completely forgive the wasted version of me, but the recovery version of me was too much to forgive. For sure, I was still an asshole to her as a sober person, but I do feel like I conducted myself with way more integrity. I was open and honest—too open and honest, as it turned out. It was the real me that Kat didn't like.

There is some additional irony in me explaining how Kat's fundamental need for privacy doomed the relationship and that explanation being *in a book*. That will be published. And hopefully widely read. I can chalk that up to being true to the person I really am, or I can concede that is me still being the same asshole who Kat couldn't stomach being with. I suppose both are true.

*   *   *

After things went south with Kat, I went on a European tour, and the sexual sobriety that I'd worked so hard on for years went out the fucking window. I was acting out like crazy.

My good buddy Scott Randolph was with me for those Europe dates. I had hired him originally to help me maintain my sexual sobriety on the road. He was a recovering alcoholic and sex addict—a double winner, as we sometimes call it—so he knew the terrain. We'd share hotel rooms every night, and on previous tours, he was essentially a professional cock-blocker. On that European tour, not so much.

Scott and I both fell off the sexual sobriety wagon. In a way, that sort of made it easier to do the wrong thing. This is a truism for sobriety of any kind: If you've got two people who are trying to stay sober and one of them loses it, the sober person is almost never going to lift up the relapsing person. It's always the other way around—the relapser drags the sober person down with him. That's why in 12-step programs, they always tell you that if you're going to carry a message of sobriety to a no-longer sober person, *do not go alone*. By yourself, you are far more likely to get sucked into that vortex with your buddy than to pull him or her out. As much as you may want to, you can't go into the darkness to help people. You've got to stay in the light.

Well, Scott and I were very much in the darkness. And it sucked. I mean, as I already went into detail about in the previous chapter, the whole sexual bender thing is fun for a minute, but it starts feeling awful pretty quickly. This time it descended into unmanageable chaos. I was deceitful with lots of women, I was stressed out, and I felt hugely guilty about all of it. This was no fucking way to live.

When the tour ended, I got myself back on the straight and narrow, and I was determined to stay there. I knew if I was going to have any chance at a real, functioning long-term relationship, if I was ever going to find someone who would tolerate me into my old age (and maybe even love me?), I had to be deliberate about every step of the process.

In January 2017, I was contacted about making a stunt video for social media that would help promote the Pepsi/Papa John's Super Bowl Halftime show. Now, we haven't really gotten into this yet, but I have a lot of food issues. Because of course I do. I have a real problem with sugar. And flour. And condiments. We will dive into the humiliating extent of my food issues soon enough, but one consistent thing in my diet is that I don't drink any fucking soda. I mean, I used to guzzle that shit when I was younger, but for the past twelve years, at least, soda has been nothing but straight garbage for me. I also haven't eaten any meat other than fish for more than thirteen years. So Pepsi and Papa John's don't exactly align with my diet, not to mention my morality. But, candidly, they offered me $30,000 to make this video, so I did it. Yes, that's how much my morals could be bought for in 2017: a cool thirty grand. I'm not proud of it.

The sponsors pumped a lot of money into the production for this video too. There was a full professional crew, a soundstage, and they'd even hired three models to be there hanging around looking hot. I wasn't really into the models, though. It was a woman working in the art department who had dressed the set who caught my eye. Her name was Lux, and she was gorgeous and funny. I felt a spark between us, but she was also wearing a ring on her wedding finger, so I kept a respectful distance.

A little more than a week later, though, Lux slid into my DMs. I was stoked. It turns out the ring was just a tool to keep creepy dudes from hitting on her. I guess the fact that I hadn't hit on her meant that I was not a creepy dude and thus had cleared the first hurdle. We made a plan to go to a vegan restaurant together a few days later.

It didn't take me long to suss out that Lux was different from most of the women I'd dated. And *good* different. On that first date, she had this incredible energy. She was excited and enthusiastic telling me about *other* people in her life. She had recently gone to great expense and much trouble to surprise her best friend with a trip to Japan. Her friend was working multiple jobs, had two kids, was exhausted, and had never traveled anywhere. So Lux called her friend's bosses to get her time off, arranged childcare, booked them this trip to Japan, and paid for everything. The way she talked about it with such unbridled delight was something I hadn't often seen. She arguably couldn't afford it, but she was lit up with the joy of giving, of doing something for someone else. She also mentioned how she had gone into debt to pay for a ridiculously expensive back surgery for her dog. Her dog needed the operation, and Lux couldn't conceive of *not* doing it. It was so clear from that first date that Lux was a rare thing: a genuinely good person. It was infectious.

I wanted to be wary of my previous history of burning through relationships, so it was a whole week before we went out again. I was no less enamored with her. But I was very careful to go slowly. I was honest with Lux about having a fucking dreadful track record in this department. I described to her my pattern of getting infatuated, having an intense physical attraction, and then once I had sex, an invisible switch flipped and I'd lose interest. I didn't want to repeat this pattern with her. So we were careful. We didn't even kiss for the first month we dated.

But then, on Super Bowl Sunday, we went for a hike and then out for sushi. We shared our first kiss at that sushi bar while watching the Super Bowl, which, yes, is maybe not the most romantic first kiss of all time, but so what. (Interesting side note: Pepsi never used that Super Bowl stunt video I made. They deemed it too violent and disturbing. So, for betraying my morals, I got thirty grand and met Lux, and in return, Pepsi got nothing from me. Further proof that there is no justice in this world.)

After making out at that sushi bar, we went back to my house and got a little more intimate but didn't have sex yet. We were lying in my bed, and I remember asking Lux, "How long can I keep you?" She moved in with me pretty much immediately afterward.

I know, I know, I know. *But, Steve, what about your plan to be deliberate and careful? What happened to taking it slowly?* My answer to that is two-fold. First, mind your own fucking business. Just kidding. I've long lived by the credo that my business is *everybody's* business, whether they want to hear about it or not. But to be fair, the circumstances were a little unique. Lux had been in a long-term relationship with a guy, and when that relationship soured, her living situation got very precarious. She needed to get a new place, and she *did* get her own apartment. But all that happened right as our relationship was ramping up. I don't think she ever spent a night in that apartment. She wanted to get it to make sure she wasn't putting any undue pressure on our relationship, but we ended up just calling that place "the storage unit" because that's pretty much all it was for her.

The funny thing is, unlike with Kat or some of my other previous girlfriends, on paper, Lux and I weren't necessarily a great match. She wasn't famous and didn't have a real public profile. There is a pretty huge income disparity between us. She's not a vegan or a vegetarian. She's not sober or in recovery. She's exceedingly normal. I am exceedingly not.

But relationships don't happen on paper, they happen in the real world. And in the real world, there is something about Lux and me that works. We laugh at the same things. We believe in the same things. Most people hate rats, but when we discovered that the bird feeders right outside the sliding glass door of our bedroom were attracting rats at night, we loved it. In fact, we were mindful to buy extra birdseed so every last critter would have enough to eat.

Lux and I complement each other too. One of our favorite little pastimes is doing those Mensa-type quizzes together. You can find these sorts of IQ tests all over the internet. What's interesting about us is that, separately, we score pretty lousy. Individually, we're basically morons. But when we do those quizzes together, we kill it. We fill in each other's gaps. We're good together.

Being good together doesn't mean we don't have problems. We've got lots. But they don't become loud arguments. Look, I have a tendency to suck up all the oxygen in any room I'm in. As a hot chick, Lux has struggled with suddenly being in a relationship where everyone is looking at me and not her. But she's such a selfless person that she's more likely to help me get more attention rather than try to deflect some of it onto herself. Whereas I've been with women who tolerate my spotlight-hogging, she may be the first who actively facilitates it.

I think some of that comes from working in production for so long as an art director and production designer. She's used to her work enhancing someone else's. With any of the stunts or videos I do, she's not just quietly supporting my lunacy, she's aiding and abetting it. When I told her that I wanted to start collecting urine in bottles and keeping them around our house for a stunt I was planning, she would've been well within her rights to object to living for months among bottles of piss. Instead, she started peeing in bottles too. That's how she rolls.

When we set up a shoot for the opening sequence of my

second comedy special, *Gnarly*, I was duct-taped to the side of a truck, and Johnny Knoxville began hitting baseballs at me. I was defenseless up there on the truck, completely immobilized by the tape. After a few balls, Lux stepped in.

"Whoa, whoa, whoa," she said to Knoxville. "That's it! You're done! You've got to stop!" For a moment, I thought she just couldn't stand to see her man getting hurt. As it turned out, that wasn't the problem at all. She was worried that he was going to hit one of the cameras with a baseball.

When I decided to do snow angels in flaming rocket fuel on our living room floor during a dry, hot summer in the Hollywood Hills, she was the one who was mindful enough to go around closing all the doors to the house so the smoke wouldn't billow out, alerting the neighbors or the fire department and shutting down the shoot. Never mind that our home was filling with smoke and I was on *fire*!

Then there's the moment in my Bucket List show that I point to and credit for confirming beyond a doubt that Lux was the girl for me. I was filming a stunt I'd thought about for a long time: I wanted to see what happened when shit really hit a fan. We bought a big industrial fan, and I squatted over it while Lux held the video camera. At the moment of impact, as my shit literally began to fly, a couple other friends who were there all went scrambling for cover. Lux was no less disgusted than any of them, but while they ran away, she moved closer to me. Her primary concern—even more than dealing with the pieces of my actual feces that had peppered her bare legs—was making sure we got the footage. *That's* my girl.

All that said, Lux is not a "yes person." I mean, she's definitely facilitated all sorts of things that a lot of sensible people would have no fucking part of, but she also knows when to step in and say, "Fuck that. That's not happening." She's shut down stunt ideas before they got started. In fact, her willingness to do that is what makes her approval so credible.

We all need partners in our lives who make us better versions of ourselves, people who bring out the best and help minimize the worst. It's not about trying to "fix" someone or push them to improve themselves. All that stuff should happen organically. That's what Lux is for me, and what I think I am for her.

*   *   *

One of the larger potential land mines we've sidestepped in our relationship is money. There is no getting around the fact that I make a lot more of it than Lux does. This is not necessarily an uncommon dynamic in relationships. When one person makes more than the other, it can cause an imbalance in what is supposed to be a partnership of equals. Frequently, people will choose to ignore it, to not talk about it. Don't poke the eight-hundred-pound gorilla in the room. But eventually, if you don't pay attention to that gorilla, it's going to start tearing shit up.

Talking about money is always awkward. But I think not talking about it is way worse. When we first started dating, Lux would always insist on paying for things. But there was a point where her paying for things didn't make much sense to me. As our relationship progressed I had to say to Lux, "Hey, we live in a world fucked-up enough that idiots like me get paid a lot more than people who actually do important work. Having money doesn't make me a better person. If anything, it makes me a worse one. I respect the hell out of you for always trying to pay for everything, and the last thing I ever want to do is deprive you of your dignity, but kindly take your hand off the bill. I'm paying for dinner."

Lux was not and is not looking for a free ride. She doesn't want to be someone's trophy wife. She's independent. She still works constantly and loves what she does. I watch her climbing the ladder of production design knowing that, at some point, when my shtick gets old, when the world tires of me, we may be leaning more heavily on her income.

We maintain separate bank accounts, but after we got engaged in 2018, we opened our books to each other. She could see how much money I had and I could see what she'd saved. There were going to be no secrets, no budding resentments about money. She also made it clear that we should have a prenuptial agreement. I never brought it up. She did.

All that has helped keep our relationship on an even keel. Lux doesn't hesitate to tell me to clean my fucking dishes and put them in the dishwasher simply because I paid for them and the house they're in. And that's how it should be. I'm looking for a partner in life, not an employee. That doesn't mean things don't still occasionally get weird with money, but the longer we're together, the less weird it is.

*　　*　　*

Probably the only thing that sinks more relationships than money is sex. These are the great taboos that society has told us we're only supposed to whisper about. But I'm not good at whispering.

Lux understood pretty much from day one about my sex

addiction issues. As much as I feared repeating the patterns of past relationships, those patterns gave me a well-worn road map of treacherous hazards to avoid. As my sex life with Lux heated up, I was bracing for the inevitable moment when it cooled off, when sex was no longer as exciting as it was at the start.

I'd like to say that because of our deep spiritual and emotional bond, and the thoughtful way that we were conducting our relationship, that the cooling off never happened, that we kept fucking like horny jackrabbits forever, but that's not true. It's probably unnecessary and maybe even inappropriately personal for me to get really graphic about this, but you wouldn't be reading this book if you didn't want to hear unnecessary, inappropriately personal and graphic things from me. Early on in my relationship with Lux, there were times when I couldn't get it done sexually. My dick wasn't staying hard, and that wasn't fun for either one of us. As much as women might say, "It's okay. It happens to all guys"—and I don't doubt that it does—it's still painful. For Lux, it was like me biologically telling her she's not beautiful or sexy. It sucks.

Normally, this would be the point in a relationship when I'd start looking for a way out. But I didn't want to let sex blow up this relationship, so I leaned hard into the real connection I have with Lux.

It's important to accept that there are peaks and valleys in a sex life, even with—*especially* with—someone you love. If there have been moments with Lux when my libido has dipped, when I couldn't stay hard or couldn't finish, inevitably, the next time we had sex after that, it would be explosive. So just be patient with your dick. Or your partner's.

Also—and I hesitate to say this—but I'd be remiss if I didn't mention that Lux getting a boob job, which she did in 2020, did wonders for my boner. Now, this is delicate ground to tread on, and when Lux was first talking about getting her boobs enlarged, I was very careful to toe a line: I was supportive but otherwise agnostic about the whole venture. I had no problem with her original titties. I love all of her. But this was something she'd wanted for a while, so who was I to stand in the way of her dream? When it happened, though, I found that I was *very* into her new boobs. Maybe it's sort of like when your partner gets a new haircut and then sex suddenly feels new and different. Granted, unlike haircuts, which can happen every couple of months, boob jobs are kind of a one-time deal. So I'm not sure I'd recommend them as a long-term cure for a sexual slump.

Sex can feel like an existential puzzle at times. For men, I do believe there is a biological imperative that is constantly at odds with our social and emotional imperatives. It is built into men's DNA to want "strange." We are programmed to spread our seed far and wide, to pass on our genes to as many partners as are willing to take them on board. That is my way of trying to put an intellectual, scientific spin on men's primal desire to fuck lots of different chicks.

I'd be lying if I said that sex with one person, even if it's the person I want to be with forever, is as consistently stimulating as sex with lots of people. But that's just the biology talking. The trade-off is completely worth it. That life of humping everything that moves is exciting, but for me, it's also unbelievably stressful, guilt-ridden, depressing, and time-consuming. (Yes, I know it sounds trivial to point out, but chasing pussy is a humongous time suck.) I can't be single and have sex with multiple partners and feel good about myself. I've tried that and it doesn't work for me. But knowing that, for more than five years now, I've been in a loving relationship with this person who makes me laugh, who challenges me, who I am deeply bonded with, and I haven't fucked it up by sticking my dick anywhere it doesn't belong, makes me feel good about *myself.* It makes me feel good about who I am. (I mean, you knew it was all going to come back to *me* in the end, right?)

Here's the thing that I can see now but would never have been able to understand years ago: All those messy, painful relationships I had when I was younger, all the shit I was doing to fuck up those relationships, made me ready to be in the relationship that I'm in now, the one that—unless I'm jinxing it by saying so—feels like it's going to last. Now, smarter people than me, more empathetic people than me, more thoughtful people, more selfless people, probably don't need forty-plus years of fucking up to figure their shit out. Maybe you can learn from the example of the dumb fucks like myself and do it in half the time. Or maybe it's something you've got to stumble through on your own.

In most of my past relationships, I was looking for someone to fix me, to make me happy, to sort my fucking mess of a life out. I realize now that it wasn't until I started to do those things for myself that I had any chance of being in a successful, fulfilling relationship.

I will share this one other piece of wisdom about relationships that I believe is universal. Any healthy relationship is based on two people *not* needing each other. I know that there are millennia worth of love songs that have been trying to convince you of the exact opposite thing, but when you feel like you *need* to be with someone, that they are absolutely vital to your functioning as a human being, that may sound romantic, but it's fucking doomed. That's not love, that's codependence. Two people who are relying on each other for their happiness or well-being are not good for each other. If you feel like you're going to fall apart without someone, well, one day, you're probably going to fall apart.

I dare say too that when you learn to be in a healthy relationship with someone, the rest of your life—work, friendships—often seems to come together. Mine did, anyway. Only after I got together with Lux did I truly start killing it in other areas of my life. It seems that once you get your heart and your dick moving in the right direction, the rest of you is eager to follow.

4

Whatever You Have Never Feels Like Enough (But That's Okay)

I love calendars. I fantasize sometimes about having a whole room in my house that is wallpapered with them. These wouldn't be run-of-the-mill calendars that you might find in a souvenir shop. No, these would be *my* calendars. They would be on permanent display as a record of exactly how busy I've been.

As it is, I have that stuff on my iPhone in an app called Awesome Cal that allows me to go crazy with color-coding. My comedy tour is in green. Production work is in red, but shoots are in white. Releases of digital content are purple, but episodes of my podcast are brown. Publicity obligations are gray. Recovery stuff is pink. Physical self-care is in yellow. Things I do for fun are in orange. And any other shit that I consider to be a pain in the ass but which doesn't fall into any of these other categories is blue. I absolutely love swiping back through past months and looking at everything I've already completed. In fact, I'm such a psycho about it that if I do something that wasn't in my calendar—a last-minute business call, an impromptu video shoot or skateboard session—I will go back and put it in my calendar just to give myself credit for doing it. To look back at those months filled with a wash of reds and blues and greens and yellows and purples is a way of confirming my view of myself as a guy who *gets shit done*. If it goes in my calendar, it happens. I figure if I love looking at all that in my phone so much, imagine being surrounded by it, in a room in my house. It would be a literal manifestation of my happy place.

When I think about why my calendars make me so happy, I'm reminded of the epilogue at the end of the previous book I wrote. It was titled "What Comes Next." There was no question mark at the end of that title, which wasn't a mistake. It was a creative choice. Because it's the question mark that fucks me up. That whole epilogue was an exercise in assessing where my life was headed, what I had coming up. At the time, I had a few things in the works, but the conclusion was, at some point I was going to have to be okay with the idea that eventually *nothing* comes next. That one day there wouldn't be a next job, a next stunt, a next show, and I was going to have to find a way to live with that without freaking the fuck out. The joy I get from my calendars is overwhelming evidence that more than a decade on from writing that epilogue, I'm not much closer to being okay with nothing coming next. My calendar is one way I manage that existential anxiety. As long as I'm able to keep filling it up with that glorious, fucked-up rainbow of constant activity, I know I'm good. At least for the time being.

I read somewhere that all our motivations in life come down to one of two things: love or fear. I believe that, and I have to admit, mine are frequently the latter. I fear being forgotten. I fear going broke. Believe it or not, I fear being embarrassed. I fear decrepitude. I fear falling face-first into a pile of cocaine, fucking a random fan, catching some gnarly STD, and then burning my life to the ground. My calendars are just one way to manage those fears, and a check against them ever coming to fruition. Which is pretty good for a little iPhone app.

Perhaps I should've figured out a way to shed all this gnawing anxiety before sitting down to write the world's next great self-help book. But I don't think ridding your life of anxiety is a realistic goal. You've just got to keep it from ruining your life. And to do that, it helps to understand it better.

I spent the first part of my life trying to get things. Frankly, I'm still trying to get things. I think most of us are the same way. The main thing I've always wanted was attention. The booze, the drugs, the girls, the stunts, the shows, whatever—most everything I've ever done was done to get more people looking at me. I know it's not the healthiest or most flattering motivation, but, hey, that's me. If you look at just how much of the world's economy is driven by advertising, I suspect that attention might actually be the most valuable commodity known to man. So, of all the character defects that I could be driven by, perhaps, in some way, I got lucky. Your motivations may be different, and I don't doubt that you're a healthier, happier person if they are.

What I've found—and what a lot of people find, I think—is that as soon as I get the things I want, they never feel like enough. Even the things that I live for these days—like, say, one of my YouTube videos getting millions of views the first day I publish it—never fixes me. It just makes me feel anxious about how my next video will perform.

Then there are the material things. I think plenty of people can relate to being unreasonably excited about buying something—maybe a sexy new camera or the latest iPhone—only for it to feel like boring old news the second they've torn the packaging open. If you saw how much dumb shit I've bought on Amazon, you'd know that I have some serious growing to do in that department. None of these acquisitions leads to long-term satisfaction or contentment. It all just leads to wanting more, more, more.

Buddhists believe that all human suffering results from craving and that we should strive to eliminate craving from our lives. That shit makes perfect sense to me. Let's say you rupture your eardrum, much like I did not too long ago when my buddy fired a T-shirt cannon full of dog shit at my face from two feet away. It hurts like a motherfucker, and you crave for that pain to end. At the opposite end of the spectrum, if you experience some sort of pleasure, if you eat a Snickers or get featured on TMZ for doing a backflip off a bridge into a river in San Antonio, you immediately crave more of it. That craving of wanting pleasure to last longer and become more intense is not fundamentally different than the craving for pain to lessen and come to an end. What the Buddhists are saying is that no matter what our situation is, it's our craving for it to improve that causes suffering. Some of us—like me—are more susceptible to our cravings than others. So, one Snickers, one beer, one line of blow, one article on TMZ, one naked girl—none of them are ever enough.

But to bring it back to the Buddhists for a second, the point is to *strive* to eliminate craving. To try. They teach that the way to end suffering is to cultivate acceptance of all things being exactly the way they are. Of course, I don't think it's possible for any of us to eliminate craving altogether. But by understanding our cravings, by recognizing them and working on preventing them from controlling our lives, we're getting closer to being okay with who we are and our place in the universe, which seems like a pretty worthwhile goal. I have no doubt that actual Buddhists are cringing at my two-paragraph summation of their twenty-five-hundred-year-old spiritual philosophy, but then again, maybe they'll find it really impressive coming from a guy who fills T-shirt cannons with dog shit.

*   *   *

When I first quit the drinking and drugging in 2008, the world was undergoing a major financial crisis. (I don't think there was any connection between the two events, but, hey, I'm not an economist.) Most people are surprised to find out that I hadn't already pissed away every cent I had when I was constantly wasted, but back then, I'd simply never given a shit about buying stuff other than drugs.

Up to that point, I had always managed my money the same way I had managed the rest of my life: with utter neglect. I had a business manager who received payments on my behalf for all the work I did, and I trusted my dad, a former corporate executive, along with this New York stockbroker dude, to manage my money in any way they saw fit. Aside from occasionally opening emails to read only the very bottom line of my quarterly financial statements, I paid zero attention to my money. But when that global financial meltdown happened, I got beat up pretty badly. The majority of my money had been in the stock market, and all of those investments fucked me. I lost more than half of everything I'd saved.

That would've hardly even bothered me when I was younger. I was so sure I'd be dead before I was thirty that planning for the future, thinking about what comes next, wasn't in my field of vision. But having just gotten sober, I was taking care of myself and my health for the first time. My life was filled with uncertainty. My career prospects were questionable at best. I was worried that my earnings potential could fall off a cliff at any moment. In fact, I had no way of knowing that it hadn't *already* fallen off a cliff. Then suddenly there's this financial crisis that I barely understand, and—poof!—just like that, half my money is gone. I may have never cared much about money, but when I saw so much of it disappear right as my life expectancy seemed to be increasing dramatically, I suddenly gave way more of a shit. In fact, I became consumed with anxiety about money, about my career, about losing the rest of what I had. Maybe I'd never get another job in the entertainment world again. Then what was I going to do? I wasn't qualified to do much except act like an asshole in front of a camera, and even though I didn't live lavishly by any stretch of the imagination, I got shit-scared of going broke and staying that way for the many decades I could have left to live.

I knew, logically, that there were people in far, far worse financial straits, but logic doesn't really play a part in all this. It's that damn craving problem. There have been surveys done of people who have tens of millions of dollars in the bank and feel like they're financially insecure. No reasoned economic analysis or profit-and-loss statement will change their mind. Nothing is more addictive than wealth. It's not that different from a need to drink or a compulsion to fuck or an inability to stop shoving chocolate cake in your mouth. You can't reason with your cravings.

This all helps explain how I let Russell Brand talk me into taking a course in Transcendental Meditation, though, truth be told, I think Russell Brand could've talked me into sticking my dick in a blender. The dude can talk. But I was desperate for something to alleviate my anxiety. I bought into the idea that craving was at the root of all suffering—mine and others'—and, philosophically, I could wrap my head around meditation being the key to letting go of that. If I'm being totally honest, I also looked at all the super-famous, incredibly successful people who swore by TM and thought, *Shit, there must be some secret to it. I need to get in on this.* I imagine a lot of people have gotten into Scientology for similar reasons.

Anyway, Russell introduced me to an incredibly sweet lady who is known as one of the best TM teachers in the world, yet, for some reason, meditation was really hard for me. I couldn't sit still, and trying to made me so uncomfortable that it felt like I was having panic attacks. I kept trying, and even though I didn't feel like it was working for me, the very process of trying made me feel better. Just putting in the work, even if it felt like I was getting nothing substantial out of it, built my self-esteem. *I wasn't a quitter.* My acceptance of the fact that I sucked at meditating was kind of the most Zen thing about the whole process.

This meditation teacher I was working with was affiliated

with the David Lynch Foundation. If you haven't heard of it, the foundation was started by the famed *Twin Peaks* and *Blue Velvet* director to spread the gospel of TM. The place is a bit of a celebrity circle-jerk—when you go to their center in L.A. where they teach meditation, the walls are filled with photos of wildly famous TM practitioners—which, on one level, I found really distasteful, but which, on another level, of course totally appealed to me. Anyway, one of their big pushes is to introduce TM to troubled, disadvantaged kids in L.A. They see it as a way to disrupt the school-to-prison pipeline. Even though I was struggling to make TM work for me, it seemed like a worthy enough cause, so I decided to help raise money for it.

As with everything, once I'm in, I'm *all* in, so for months I pushed this fundraiser hard. I blabbed about it all the time. I posted stuff all over my social media and created a raffle that encouraged my fans to donate the most money they could. The grand prize was an all-expense-paid trip to be a VIP guest at the taping of what was going to be my first comedy special on Showtime. I raised something like $20,000, which, for the amount of shilling I was doing, was actually kind of pathetic, but, hey, it's still twenty grand that I sent to the David Lynch Foundation.

In return, the foundation didn't so much as even thank me. In fact, they never even acknowledged the money I raised at all. Here I was thinking that maybe I'd get my photo on the wall between Paul McCartney and Jerry Seinfeld or something, and instead I got jack shit. They didn't even follow me back on Twitter. The message I got was that they considered me too toxic for their image. They were fine with taking the money I raised but would have nothing to do with me in public. It drove me fucking nuts that they wouldn't let me into their little club. I know it shouldn't have, and I know it makes me look like a shallow dickhead for saying so, but I couldn't help myself. I became so consumed with resentment that I decided to do something about it: I quit meditating. Out of spite. Because, you know, *fuck them*.

Now, look, don't think that I don't see the irony here. I get that the whole point of Transcendental Meditation and Buddhism is to eliminate craving and learn to give of yourself without the expectation of getting something in return. Shit, maybe if I was better at meditating, it wouldn't have bothered me so much. But it did. What can I say? I want the credit. I'm superficial. That's me. On a fundamental level, groping desperately for other people to recognize me is a unifying strand of my DNA. I don't care what David Lynch, Russell Brand, or the fucking Dalai Lama says about it, fighting who you really are is not going to lead to existential satisfaction or enlightenment. Well, at least not for me. No matter how devout I become in any spiritual practice, no matter how well I work the twelve steps, I will always be, on some level, the asshole who wants everyone looking at him all the time. I accept that, and accepting that has made me a much more content human being. So, you know, namaste, motherfucker.

*   *   *

Although I was sufficiently freaked by the financial crisis, I didn't suddenly become a savvy money manager. Because even sober, chastened, and relatively panicked about my uncertain career prospects, I was still even worse at investing than you would expect a guy who stuck a leech to his eyeball to be.

I continued listening to Dad about money stuff, and post–financial crisis, he'd really come to believe that the whole economic system in the United States was a pyramid scheme, destined to fail spectacularly. I bought into this doomsday thinking, and as such, started buying gold. I bought lots of it, at what turned out to be grossly inflated prices, which, of course, soon plummeted back to earth. I also bought a house in 2014, long after real-estate prices had skyrocketed from record lows following the financial crisis. I love the shit out of my house, but it kills me to think of how different my financial situation would be right now if I'd bought it three or four years earlier, instead of buying all that stupid fucking gold.

I've come to believe that I am simply a cursed investor. Maybe in the depths of my addiction, I made some sort of spiritual pact with the universe, or maybe, before I was even born, it was predetermined that I would never achieve obscene wealth. Perhaps this pact is protecting me. I mean, who knows what kind of trouble I might get into if I had Johnny Knoxville's money? I almost don't want to know.

Whatever the reason, it feels as though if I invest in anything, the very act of my investing in it dooms the investment. By the same token, if I decide *not* to invest in something, I expect that business is going to take off. Sadly, I suspect the most solid financial advice I can offer is to follow my investing decisions and simply do the exact opposite of whatever I do. You're welcome.

Amid all my bad investment decisions and cloudy financial future, I did find one surefire source of income: stand-up. I remember, not long after I first committed myself to doing stand-up, I got an offer from Carolines, a big comedy club in New York City, to come headline six shows over the course of four days for $20,000. It turned out that this wasn't just a mistake on this one club's part. Soon, similar offers rolled in from other clubs, and just like that, I was a touring stand-up.

On one level, I recognize how ridiculously lucky I was to find this source of income that, at least at first, I really didn't deserve. On another level, it wasn't long before I was struggling with the monotonous existence of being a touring stand-up. Every week would be the same: I'd spend endless hours in airports and on planes, only to arrive at hotels super late at night, get next to no sleep, then have to race to and from radio stations at the crack of dawn to answer the same awkward questions over and over, all so I could perform the same show six times in the same room. Rinse and repeat.

I know I have no right to complain about this. These are uptown problems. I know thousands of comics are grinding it out at bullshit gigs for no money and would love to have this life that I'm bitching about. I'm sure those same comics would read these last two paragraphs and want to kick the shit out of me. After all, I got to essentially skip the line. Maybe I'd appreciate the perks of being a headliner a little more if I knew how thankless it is to do comedy when you aren't one. But my reality can only be my reality. And I'm telling you, any touring comic who claims to love the *Groundhog Day* lifestyle of the comedy club circuit is either lying or considerably more mentally ill than I am.

As much as I didn't really like the mind-numbing repetition of life on the road as a stand-up, I was deathly afraid of leaving that money on the table. Who knew how long this gravy train would keep rolling, and the last thing I wanted to do was to look back one day, while I was a washed-up nobody living in abject poverty, and regret turning up my nose at people willing to pay me to get onstage. I was determined to make as much money as I could while the getting was good.

During my first year on the comedy club circuit, I watched along with the rest of the world as Charlie Sheen was going through a very public and protracted meltdown. He had gotten fired from his hit TV show, *Two and a Half Men*, and was unbelievably fucked up on drugs. It seemed like every day, he'd show up on some radio station or website blabbing about how he was a warlock with tiger blood, or a bitchin' rock star from Mars, or trashing his former employers and co-stars. Each of those interviews got picked up by every media outlet under the sun, making Charlie Sheen arguably the most famous guy in the world at that time. The magnitude of the spectacle was profound, and, unlike my drug-induced meltdown, which convinced my friends to force me into rehab, Charlie booked a tour with his.

The tour that Charlie went on was just a rolling fucking train wreck. He didn't have any sort of act that he did onstage, but people lined up around the block to see the wreckage. His catchphrase "Winning!" became a cultural touchstone. He got more famous for being a fuckup than he'd ever been for being a successful actor. I was more than three years sober at the time, but it probably tells you all you need to know about the headspace I was in that as I watched Charlie fall apart in public, my main takeaway was "Man, he's really onto something with this!" When I saw Charlie promoting and monetizing his drug-fueled demise, I actually contemplated a deliberate relapse of my own. You know, for business reasons.

I'm kind of not kidding. Charlie sold out a nationwide tour of huge theaters with one crazy tweet announcing he was taking his shit show on the road, while I was mostly struggling to fill small comedy clubs. Nobody seemed to care that I was clean and sober. Maybe the stage was set for me to blow up even bigger than Charlie if I followed in his footsteps and made every effort to let it rip even harder than he did.

That plan might have been the ultimate expression of my anxiety about going broke and being forgotten. Among the many bad ideas that have crossed the transom of my mind over the years, it's got to be the absolute worst. But my first addiction was always to the spotlight, so it makes perfect sense that it would be the spotlight that would threaten to take everything away from me again. Fortunately, this was one idea I did not follow through on.

*   *   *

When I gave up on Transcendental Meditation, I did so out of spite, to stick it to the David Lynch Foundation, not that the David Lynch Foundation ever had any idea about the grudge I held against them. It was all quiet seething on my part. But my failure with TM, and especially the way I quit on it, bothered me. None of the issues that I'd been hoping to address with TM had been dealt with, and in fact, I truly believed my quality of life was suffering from the way I gave up on it.

In 2019, I finally decided to do something about it. No, I didn't make peace with the David Lynch Foundation and devote myself to somberly practicing TM. Fuck those guys. Instead, I took up something called Vedic meditation. Now, if you want to know the difference between Transcendental and Vedic meditation, the best I can discern is that there's no fucking difference whatsoever, yet somehow the two camps are at low-grade war with each other. The Vedic people actually talk shit about TM and vice versa, so aligning myself with the Vedics nurtured my grudge, which got me extra motivated to go all in on it.

I think the thing that finally pushed me over the edge to give Vedic meditation a try was a sober buddy of mine named Adam Jablin, who had gotten in the habit of screenshotting his meditation app and sending it to me. It would show that he'd meditated for something like six hundred days in a row, which I thought was rad. In fact, it made me jealous. I wanted that shit on my iPhone too. So yeah, resentment, spite, jealousy—these were the petty inducements that inspired me to commit myself to this deeply spiritual practice.

I went to a new meditation teacher, who gave me a new mantra, and I was off and running. I stopped giving myself a hard time about how I approached meditating. If I felt restless, or my mind was overly active, I wouldn't shame myself for it. I'd just recognize the feelings or thoughts and return my focus to the mantra. Once I finished, I wouldn't grade the meditation or try to figure out how I could do it better next time. The focus was no longer on whether I was doing it well; it was just on whether I was doing it at all.

And I haven't stopped doing it since. Not for one single day. The first thing I do when I wake up in the morning is meditate. I do it again at night, usually around dinner or before bed. Whatever happens, I never skip a session. It's gotta be twice, every single day. I use a meditation app, just like my buddy Adam, to time and keep a record of each of my meditations, even though a lot of meditation teachers frown on that. But for me, it's necessary. In fact, I sometimes wonder if it's the whole point. As I write this sentence, I've maintained an average of forty-one minutes a day for more than six hundred and fifty days in a row. Every time I check in with my new meditation teacher to let him know I'm still keeping the streak alive, he's fucking stoked. Using the app to track and record all this gives me incentive not to break the streak. And you know how much I love streaks. It's no different from my calendar app. I cling to the credit it gives me for getting things done. I'm actually terrified of breaking the streak. It's as if the pettiness that first drew me to Vedic meditation has persisted in perpetuity. Some might see that as totally undermining the point of the meditation, but I don't give the slightest fraction of a fuck.

Meditation has given me some tangible benefits. One of them is simply training me to have discipline and focus. The very act of sitting still and being quiet for forty-one minutes a day is a hell of a lot harder than you might think, particularly for someone like me. So being able to do that, every day, no matter what, takes real discipline. Just checking that off my to-do list every day makes me feel good. Now, don't think I don't recognize that I'm breaking my arm patting myself on the back for sitting around and doing nothing for forty-one minutes a day. But I don't give a fuck about that either. It makes me feel good.

I first started this daily meditation streak at the very end of

2019. The following year COVID-19 shut down the world. We were all confined to our houses, economies cratered, there was widespread suffering and death. Knowing what I've already told you about my anxieties and my compulsions, you would think that I would've become a nerve-racked basket case in 2020. Instead, I had arguably my best year ever. I know that's a shitty thing to say in light of all the very real human devastation that COVID has wrought, but it's true. I did well financially, spiritually, and emotionally. I didn't freak out about my health. I didn't lose my shit over canceled tours or the *Jackass* production being shut down. Unlike the financial crisis of 2008, which threw me into a serious tailspin, I just kind of took all the disruptions that came with COVID in stride. I credit meditation for a lot of that.

It's nothing I can really prove, but I suspect that a disciplined meditation practice helps cultivate focus in other parts of your life. That's probably why so many successful people do it. I feel like it plugs me in on a spiritual level too. Not too long ago, I was talking about meditation with this vocal coach I was working with. He meditates daily too, and I told him that I thought my meditation practice causes the universe to conspire in my favor. He looked at me like I was crazy. "Huh," he said. "I never thought about that. I just do it because it calms me." But to me, that wouldn't be enough. I don't want to be calm. I want the universe conspiring in my fucking favor!

Look, on an intellectual level, I know that magic forces aren't trying to help me simply because I sit quietly and do nothing for forty-one minutes a day. But on a more ethereal, emotional level, it really feels like that's what's happening. And what good would it do me to undo that sort of magic? I've read that faith is the belief in something you don't totally understand. I guess that's what meditation is to me now. In the same way that a Christian or a Muslim or a Jew might not be able to scientifically explain why their religious practice helps them, the very belief that it does is kind of the whole ball game.

Am I telling you that you've got to meditate, that it's the key to happiness? No, I am not. All I know is that the way I've done it since 2019 has helped make my life more manageable. I'm sure there are lots of other things people do to help put structure, discipline, and balance in their lives—yoga, fasting, therapy, running marathons, journaling, long walks in the woods, jiujitsu, learning to play the bassoon, microdosing LSD—but I can only tell you what has worked for me.

Look, none of this has vanquished my anxieties from my life. I still feel a strong pull to accumulate base, material things—money, fame, work, social media followers—that are far in excess of what logic dictates I really need. My cravings haven't gone away. Yours won't either. But understanding them has kept them from wrecking my life.

When I think about that epilogue and getting okay with the idea that nothing comes next, I realize that I'll probably never be okay with it. Never ever ever. Maybe the most important thing I've learned about all this is that the work you put in trying to deal with these issues in your life can be more important than the results. In fact, often, the work *is* the result. The journey is way more important than the destination. Actually, fuck that— the journey *is* the destination.

As cliché as it sounds, one of the things that makes us human is that we are all really looking to find some sort of inner peace in our lives. And I think that's totally fine as long as we're aware that the continued search itself may very well be the closest we ever get.

5

Fuck the Greatest Hits

If you've been fortunate enough to have any sort of success in your life, there will always be pressure to just keep doing whatever it is you're doing. Some of that pressure will come from other people. If you're the star of a hit action movie, your manager, your agent, your lawyer, your financial adviser, your fans, and every movie studio in Hollywood will want you to keep starring in action movies. They will not look kindly on the buttoned-up period drama you want to do with Dame Judi Dench or the tasteful Italian clothing boutique you've always dreamed of opening. But a lot of that pressure will also be internal. Deep down, you'll know that the period drama and the boutique are risks, chances for you to fail, chances for you to confirm your own worst opinion of yourself.

This doesn't apply only to people who star in action movies. If you're an accountant, the easiest path forward is to keep being an accountant, even if what you really want to do is quit and become a pastry chef. It also doesn't apply only to your job. If you've been in any sort of relationship for an extended period of time—with a person, with a company, with a drug—you know how difficult it is to get out of that relationship, because you've often built your life around it.

In my career, I've felt this acutely. When I dropped out of college and started telling people my plans to become a "crazy-famous stuntman" with my home video camera, everyone felt sorry for me, because they knew that this was, objectively, a terrible plan. There was no precedent for this sort of thing. No one else was making a good living hurling themselves off local bridges. I'd be lying if I said I wasn't as shocked as those people were when it all worked in a big way. *Jackass* was a hit on MTV. It was a hit in movie theaters. Then I took my antics on the road and performed acts of wanton stupidity for live audiences, and they seemed to love it. The success of it all truly surpassed my wildest dreams. I mean, I knew I was ready to do some crazy-ass shit, but I never actually thought that so many people would want to see me do it.

But as the years crept by, as I quit ingesting massive amounts of narcotics, it occurred to me that there were a lot of potential long-term problems with a career built on a daily regimen of stapling my ball sack to my leg, swallowing disgusting things then vomiting them back up, and inviting wild animals to maim or kill me. I mean, putting aside the health risks, the nature of celebrity is fickle. Careers dry up and fade away quickly. Fame is a weird catch-22: Everyone wants you to keep doing the thing that they know you for while at the same time getting sick of seeing you do the thing that they know you for. The only answer, I think, is to keep trying to blaze new paths.

One of the biggest changes I've made in my career in the past fifteen years is beginning to do stand-up comedy. Now, anyone who gets into stand-up because it offers a safer work environment and more job security obviously has some serious preexisting career problems. Stand-up was a giant risk for me. There was no reason to believe that just because lots of people had always laughed *at* me that I could suddenly start making them laugh *with* me.

The first time I did stand-up, I wasn't sober. Not even close. It was 2006, and someone invited me to the Laugh Factory in L.A. to do a stunt. While I was there at the club, it occurred to me that there could be no more ballsy a stunt than to get onstage and actually attempt to do stand-up. I couldn't think of anything that would scare me more. So I sat there at the Laugh Factory trying to think of something that would manufacture some laughs, then got onstage and opened with the best thing I could come up with.

"Hey, everybody, I'm in the mood for a blowjob," I said, looking out at the crowd and then pausing momentarily. "Does anybody want one?"

It wasn't the most sophisticated joke of all time, but it was a decent little misdirection and it got a good laugh. I was only up there for a couple minutes after that, and the crowd was into it. I walked off the stage feeling amazing, and because I've never had a measured reaction to anything in my life, I immediately decided, *That's it! I'm going to be a stand-up comic!*

Before I left the club that night, I scheduled my return for a week or so later. In the interim, I spent time diligently writing material. When I came back the following week, the emcee that night was none other than Tiffany Haddish, who, at the time, was just a hardworking, largely unknown comic. She introduced me, and I bounded onstage. "I don't know if it's the amphetamines, the Xanax, the grass, or the booze, but I feel fucking great," I told the audience. And it was true. I was loaded. My set didn't really go that great, but I got a decent reaction, and in my drug-fueled, slightly delusional state, I considered it another roaring success, the next step on my eventual conquest of stand-up comedy. Jon Lovitz went up that night too, and afterward, I cornered him and asked him what he thought of my performance. He told me that I had potential but recommended that I try getting up onstage sober so that I'd actually be aware of what I was doing. That was a solid piece of advice that I completely ignored. In fact, all I heard was this legendary comic telling me, essentially, that I was a natural and could do no wrong. Once again, I scheduled my return.

As my next performance at the club approached a week later, I was brimming with narcotics and overconfidence. I was so sure I was going to kill that rather than work on the material that had done okay the previous week and try to improve it, I tossed it all out. I decided to just get up there and wing it. Because, you know, I was a fucking natural!

Holy shit, did I bomb. Even in my typically drunken state, it was mortifying. I slunk out of the club with my tail between my legs. Nonetheless, not too long after, when I was considerably more wasted, I thought it would be a good idea to go back to the club again, get onstage, and force the audience to listen to this shitty rap song I had recently recorded. It was like I had found two ways to bomb at once—musically and comedically.

I was a little chastened by all that but still hadn't learned my lesson. It wasn't long before I was back at the Laugh Factory, this time because a reality show I was shooting called *Dr. Steve-O* was scheduled to film there. Despite my previous failures, I prepared no jokes ahead of time. For some reason, it never occurred to me to revisit any of the material that had kind of worked for me during my first appearances. Once again, it did not go well. At all. The fact that this time it was being filmed by a bona fide production company and I didn't even have the benefit (or excuse) of being completely wasted made that third experience of eating shit onstage probably the most traumatizing of all.

Ultimately, that trifecta of bombing was a necessary, albeit devastating, course correction. I wouldn't so much as step foot in a comedy club for years.

Once I got sober, though, there were a limited number of things I could do with my evenings. Especially in those early days of sobriety, I had to pay attention to my intentions. My measuring stick for going anyplace for any recreational activity was based on having a legitimate reason for being there. Previously, the whole idea of "going out" meant going to bars and nightclubs to get fucked up, so now, as a sober person, that activity was a no-go. Comedy clubs felt like a fair compromise. Yes, there were people drinking there, but my purpose for being there was just to watch comedy.

I became a pretty regular fixture at the Comedy Store, the Laugh Factory, and the Hollywood Improv—as a patron. But the more nights I sat there, watching other people get laughs, the more it rankled me that I wasn't up there myself. The fact that I'd quit at the first sign of adversity ate at me. I knew that I was afraid to get back onstage, and the fact that I was letting that fear win made me feel, frankly, like a total fucking pussy. At one point, I psyched myself up enough, wrote some material, and got up again, sober, at the Laugh Factory. It went terribly, which essentially traumatized me all over again. Yet I couldn't get this idea out of my head: I wanted to be up there onstage. I felt like I *could* do it.

The root of this compulsion was the same as most everything else I do: I have a hard time being in a room where everyone isn't looking at me. I just need the external validation constantly. The idea of people paying attention to me, clapping for me, laughing at me—that kind of affirmation fills me up. It's kind of the closest I can get to a drug these days. None of this is particularly flattering to admit, but I'm long past trying to hide it.

The weird thing is, attention has always been a double-edged sword for me. I want it but I know the potential humiliation that it can bring, so I fear it too. When I was in sixth grade, I got a report card from my homeroom teacher, Mrs. Iacuessa, who absolutely nailed me in a way that is still hard for me to read. I mentioned it in my last book, but I'm going to mention it again now because it's no less applicable. She wrote, "Socially, Steve's attempt to impress his peers frequently has the opposite effect."

The dynamic Mrs. Iacuessa recognized was not much different from what happened when I bombed at stand-up. Ever since I was a kid, I wanted attention and was just flailing about for a way to get it. I yanked my own teeth out in class, I drank an entire shaker of salt, I did whatever I could think of just to get people to notice me. My hunger for the spotlight always overpowered my fears of what it might take to get that spotlight turned toward me.

I've made my career out of being this fearless guy who doesn't give a fuck what anyone thinks, but the truth is, I care *so much*. That's what made stand-up so scary for me. It's like I'm addicted to what I fear the most. I have this compulsion to make myself the center of attention, even though it terrifies me. But doing the thing that terrifies you can be both electrifying and necessary. I mean, you don't need to read a fucking self-help book to know it's important to face your fears. But it's still easier said than done.

*   *   *

In 2010, we had finished filming *Jackass 3D*, but it hadn't yet come out. I was scheduled to be interviewed by some sort of *Access Hollywood*–style show on YouTube. I arrived a little early, and the interviewer was still talking to the guy scheduled before me, Dane Cook. I didn't know Dane personally, but I knew he was a big-deal stand-up, and the producer of this show thought it would be funny if I just barged in on his interview. I didn't need a second invitation.

I crashed Dane's interview, but he wasn't the least bit flustered. I quickly turned the focus to my favorite subject: me. I mentioned that I had tried stand-up a few times before with varying degrees of success and that I wanted to try again. "Breaking bones and shoving shit up my ass isn't getting any easier," I said. He told me that I should come down to the Improv the following week and he'd get me scheduled to perform a ten-minute set. Once we got off camera, he could've easily blown me off, but he was totally serious about it. He advised me to have a few funny stories ironed out and ready to go.

Having had the experience of trying to go up there and wing it, I took his advice seriously. I spent a lot of time that next week writing and rewriting about ten minutes of material. I showed it to some friends of mine who do stand-up and got their feedback. I even went out to some hole-in-the-wall open mic room to try it out, but there were only three people in the audience, all of whom were waiting to go up onstage themselves and thus staring at their notes during my performance. It was probably no more useful than practicing my set to my dogs in my apartment. Which I also did.

When the night finally came, I went to the Improv and was fucking terrified. The two comics who went up immediately before me were Sarah Silverman and Dane, who are not easy to follow even if you're a seasoned stand-up. Which I was not. After all the insane stunts I'd done, I don't know if I've ever been as nervous for a performance as I was for this one. I had practiced my ten minutes over and over, but my set worked sequentially, so if I forgot any bit, it would all fall apart. I remember literally trembling as I got onstage. But once I got going, the ten minutes buzzed by quickly. I even heard some laughs.

Afterward, Dane took the time to sit down with me in the empty restaurant that adjoined the club, and the first thing he told me was, "All right, I'm not sending you back to the drawing board." What I heard was essentially the same thing I'd heard years earlier when I got that bit of qualified praise from Jon

Lovitz: *You're a natural and your material is amazing.* When I calmed down enough, I was able to take in some of the actual notes that Dane gave me, the main one being that I needed to calm the fuck down. It was very evident how nervous I was. A stand-up set had to feel less like a speech and more like a conversation with the audience.

Nonetheless, I left the club feeling great. At the time, Dane was at the top of the stand-up world. He'd sold out two shows at Madison Square Garden and was regularly touring arenas. If he was saying that I had a future at this, I believed that really meant something. And I took his advice. I worked on my material, and two nights later I went back up at the Laugh Factory, just before Dane's set. This time I was relaxed. Very relaxed. Suuuper relaxed. Way too relaxed, as it turned out. Afterward, Dane told me I looked almost lethargic out there. "You can't forget this is a performance," he said. "You have to be an animated version of yourself."

The next night I was back at it, adjusting the dials a bit and trying to find the happy medium. I found the process of working at it to be invigorating. It wasn't even so much the specific advice Dane was giving me that was important as much as it was the general encouragement. I didn't suck at this. I wasn't hopeless. What's kind of hilarious is that as Dane was mentoring me behind the scenes, onstage when we'd appear the same nights, he was roasting me. He'd make fun of my past drug use, my hygiene, my stand-up chops, everything. He was ruthless with me onstage, but then, off stage, a total sweetheart. This pivot didn't bother me at all. It made me feel like I belonged.

I can look back now and know that my act was not very good when I started. And when it wasn't going well onstage, it could feel awful. In some ways, bombing onstage doing stand-up is almost a perfect distillation of what it generally feels like to try anything big and new in your life. At first, it usually sucks. It's embarrassing, you sweat more than usual, and it feels like the moment will never end. When you stand onstage, tell jokes, and hope that strangers laugh, you are making yourself uniquely vulnerable. It's a similar vulnerability you feel when you apply for a new job, or ask someone out on a date, or try waterskiing for the first time: There is a decent chance that you're going to fall on your ass and end up looking like a fool. But if you learn to get comfortable with bombing—whether at stand-up, or at your new job, or with the girl you are desperately trying to charm, or on your water skis—it gradually starts sucking less and less. You realize that failure is not terminal—it's temporary. And with time and work, you improve. The more times you get comfortable with this cycle of tossing out the old and struggling with the new, the less scary it gets, and the more comfortable you will be with the messy process of change.

I think.

*   *   *

Although it took me a while to get any good at stand-up, the people who book comedy clubs didn't really give a fuck. I remember the day *Jackass 3D* came out, I went on Howard Stern to promote it and mentioned that I was now doing stand-up almost every night of the week. With the movie opening at number one at the box office, comedy clubs had apparently seen all they needed to see. I got that call I mentioned before, with an offer to headline a weekend at Carolines in New York City for $20,000. It was wildly out of proportion to the low-key, late-night sets I was doing in L.A. I felt undeserving of the offer. There were so many comics who had been slugging away for years, busting their asses, who would kill for such an opportunity. So, on principle, I decided to say no.

I'm just kidding. I totally fucking took the money without a second thought.

Around this same time, I met with a booking agent from a big agency who wanted to take me on as a client. He told me he had put out some feelers, and passed a manila envelope across the table to me. It was filled with offers similar to the one from Carolines, a stack of guarantees that totaled somewhere near $150,000. I quickly signed with the guy, and just like that, I basically had an entire stand-up tour booked.

To headline at these clubs, I was expected to perform for about an hour, which was going to be a challenge since I only had about twenty minutes of material. That first year, I supplemented my stand-up with a lot of the kind of onstage stunts and bar tricks that I'd been doing for years: fire-breathing acrobatics, squeezing lemon juice into my eyes, setting my hair on fire, balancing barstools on my chin, drinking from a glass without using my hands. To be fair, I'm sure that's what most of the people who were showing up to see me expected anyway, but it added up to a grueling physical regimen I was putting myself through every night, often two shows a night.

As for the comedy, I was definitely getting better at it, and adding more and more material to my shows, but, even to this day, I think it's fair to describe my stand-up career as a triumph over low expectations. Let's face it, when most people see me trot onstage at a comedy club, their immediate reaction is "What is this asshole doing here?" But even though there might be a legion of skeptics that I need to win over, the bar is set unbelievably low for the general public's idea of what a Steve-O stand-up show might entail. All I really need to do is not suck ass. And I am confident in telling you that I do not.

I think there's something to be said for setting reasonable expectations whenever you're trying something new. You're not supposed to be good at surfing or painting or computer programming or astrophysics the first time you try it. In fact, we have a word for people who seem to be great at everything right off the bat: assholes. Fuck those people. Take your time. But put in the work.

I remember running into Dane Cook again, back at the Laugh Factory, after having been on the road, doing headline dates for about a year. He gave me a hug and asked how I'd been doing. I couldn't contain my enthusiasm.

"Bro, since I saw you last, I've been basically touring non-stop," I told him. "I've actually performed stand-up in twelve different countries!"

He laughed and shook his head. "Man, comics must hate you."

It's an understandable assumption. I mean, stand-ups put *a lot* of stock in paying your dues, and I basically was ushered straight past all of them into headliner status before I deserved it. What I found, though, is that most comics, once they saw how seriously I was taking stand-up, once they saw that I treated my fans well, treated the club owners well, and that I wasn't a dick or a diva, didn't really hold any sort of grudge against me. Or at least if they did, they were polite enough to only talk shit behind my back and it never got back to me. Which, I suppose, is also entirely possible. Tiffany Haddish, who remembers introducing me onstage the second time I ever got up to do comedy, has always been incredibly generous with me. When I first started doing stand-up sober, she'd frequently give me tags for my jokes or just little tips. Joe Rogan has been very supportive too, as has Kevin Nealon. I remember going on Bryan Callen's podcast, and he told me that what I was doing was "authentic" and that I was "an American hero." I swear he said that. Maybe that was a little over-the-top, but he came out and said that anyone who gives me a hard time can fuck off. His words, not mine.

Still, there were a few who gave me a hard time. When I went on Marc Maron's podcast, he told me he's a purist about stand-up and that when he first saw me doing comedy, his first thought was *What the fuck? Is Steve-O doing comedy now?* And then he described what I did as "not stand-up, per se." Maron is sort of a professional curmudgeon, so this was hardly unexpected, and I truly don't think he meant it maliciously. Still, it stung a little at the time. I have often avoided calling myself a stand-up—not because I don't think what I do is stand-up, but because I know others don't see me like that. I knew people would assume I was shitty at it, and I'm too sensitive to open myself up to that criticism and trolling. Of course, if you know Maron's *WTF* podcast, it's kind of a forum for him to air his grievances and then make peace with them, so by the end of that interview, I felt like he'd kind of come around. In his parlance, "we were good."

I had a bit more of an ongoing beef with Al Madrigal, a stand-up who had been on *The Daily Show* for a while. It started around 2013. I was onstage at the Hollywood Improv, working through a new batch of material. I had just decided that I wanted to get out of my comfort zone and try all-new material, so I admit, my set that night wasn't that great, but it got some laughs. Anyway, Madrigal got up onstage after me and just laid into me. "What did we just see?" he asked the audience. "We saw Steve-O doing stand-up. Here's a guy who is taking what I feel like is my calling, something that I care about more than anything in the world, and he's using it as a last resort." He then compared me to Screech from *Saved by the Bell*. It stung.

This was different from the way Dane Cook had roasted me. Dane's jabs always felt affectionate. This felt like a pretty flagrant attack. In fact, I later discovered that when Al found out that I was on the bill that night at the Improv, he had asked to go on after me and rushed across town to do so. So it was premeditated too. After his set, he ran into me in the club and told me, "Just so you know, what you're doing isn't taken lightly."

What the fuck?

The thing is, Al was claiming to be defending the honor of stand-up, but while he was onstage attacking me, there were no jokes. No one was laughing. And what he was attacking me for was, in fact, me working on the craft of stand-up: writing new jokes, trying them out, recording the set, listening for what works. His criticism just didn't make sense.

I probably would've just let it go, but later, he went on Joe Rogan's podcast and apologized for stirring shit up with lots of other people but went out of his way to say that he didn't feel bad about what he'd said about me. Then he repeated the same insults he'd lobbed from the Improv stage. Several notable people in the stand-up community that Al claimed to be protecting actually came out publicly in my defense, including Rogan, Callen, and Bill Burr. Al and I eventually got on the phone together and hashed it out. He apologized and said that he'd heard that I was a good guy and that I wasn't treating stand-up like a lark. We're all good now, but the whole episode was probably more upsetting to me than it should've been.

The thing about trying new things in your life is that it's impossible to disentangle your ego from it all. I wish I could not care what everyone thinks about me but I do. It sucks not to be good at something, and it sucks even more not to be good at something in front of people. But with stand-up, that's part of the job. That's what makes it such a high-wire act. Working out fresh material is an amped-up version of trying anything new. You're learning in public. Your flaws are on display. Failure isn't just an option—it's a probability. But there's no other way to do it. This is how you learn to do most anything. You try. You fall down. Everyone makes fun of you for falling down. You get back up.

Someone once told me, "It's better to be a comedy factory than a comedy warehouse," and that is exactly it. The whole process of throwing out old jokes and writing new ones is really an embodiment of this chapter's title. You shouldn't rest on your laurels, mostly because it's fucking boring. When I decide to scrap jokes or stunts that are working well, it's because I'm tired of them. There's no risk. Nothing ventured, nothing gained. The process of getting onstage and doing something new is a good kind of scary. It might not work. It might bomb. The unknown is always nerve-racking. It's also thrilling. We all need that in our lives.

*   *   *

My first stand-up special, *Guilty as Charged*, had a catchy title, but it was a bit of a misnomer. The material in it loosely followed my personal autobiography but with an intense focus on my sex life and my journey through sexual addiction. Because I'm me, all that was interspersed with stunts like me getting choked unconscious by a UFC fighter, balancing a massive stepladder on my chin, and getting tased while trying to answer interview questions. You know, regular guy stuff.

As I mentioned before, all that sexual material in the first special caused major problems in my relationship with Kat Von D. By the time I started working on my second special, I was already with my fiancée, Lux, working hard on not being a full-time scumbag, so I really wanted to move away from talking constantly about my dick and all the places I've put it. I mean, I wasn't exactly becoming a clean comic, more just turning my attention to other fucked-up aspects of my life. In this case, I decided to zero in on my very checkered history with the law.

You see, I've been arrested for a lot of very dumb shit. I stapled my nut sack to my leg onstage. I swallowed a condom full of weed and smuggled it into Sweden, drug mule style. I climbed a one-hundred-and-fifty-foot crane in downtown Los Angeles carrying a small inflatable whale to protest SeaWorld. This is but a sampling of the idiocy that has landed me in jail at one time or another. As I started to put a show together that would plumb the depths of my criminal past, it occurred to me that so many of the stories behind that criminal past were captured on video. This is an ancillary benefit of pretty much having turned on a video camera when I was about fifteen and rarely turning it off since. For better or worse, I've been living in my own personal *Truman Show* for my whole adult life. A light bulb went on in my head, and it lit the way forward for this special: I'd regale the audience with tales of my entanglements with the law, and I'd augment those tales with video of the incidents.

It came together smoothly, and after touring the show for a while, I filmed the whole multimedia affair in Denver for a special, which I called *Gnarly*. At that time, Netflix was pouring resources into their comedy offerings, and in the stand-up world, getting a Netflix special had become a marker of elite status. If you had one, you were a stand-up heavyweight. I wanted that status bump badly, and I figured *Gnarly* was my ticket. I pitched it to them, but much like Al Madrigal and Marc Maron, Netflix didn't consider me a pure stand-up. They didn't buy the special.

Sadly, in the days before the explosion of streaming channels, it seemed like there was no real other place for *Gnarly*. The show was very graphic and had tons of full-frontal nudity, although not really in any sort of titillating way—unless you consider multiple shots of my wiener titillating—so it was going to be a tough sell at HBO or Showtime and had no chance someplace like Comedy Central.

I was fucking bummed. Not just that I'd spent money to film and produce *Gnarly* and wanted to recoup it, but that I had this special I was sure my fans would want to watch and couldn't figure out how to get it to them.

The answer soon presented itself: I'd just do it myself. Well, not exactly myself, so much as me and the people smarter and more talented than me who I would pay to help me. I had seen Louis C.K. set up a simple paywall on his website that allowed people to download his special, so I hired a guy, showed him Louis's website paywall, and told him essentially, "I want to do that." It worked better than I'd even hoped. I made money and put up streaming numbers that I figured would make people sit up and take notice the next time I was trying to sell a special.

From a creative standpoint, though, the longer I lived with *Gnarly*, the more something about it ate at me. The whole content of that special—and for that matter, of the first one too—was focused on *the past*. Although getting into stand-up in the first place had been a way of breaking with the past, I had slowly slid toward simply using it as a way to revel in my former glories. I was onstage talking about all the crazy shit I'd done when I was younger. Fuck, that sucks. Memory lane is a nice place to visit from time to time, but a long-term residency there feels kind of pitiful. As I started to think about putting together a new stage show, I was determined not to dwell there any longer. *Fuck the greatest hits.*

I had carved out a fairly unique act, a mixture of stand-up and stunts, but in some ways, it was unsustainable. I mean, the stuff I did onstage for *Guilty as Charged*—getting tased, getting choked out—was great, but I couldn't do that kind of shit every night. Even just the regular onstage antics I did during the early years of my comedy tours took a real physical toll. With *Gnarly*, I'd solved some of that by relying on video to show stunts I'd already done, but the downside was that I was just reliving the glory days. I didn't have to be, though: For my next tour, I decided to use the video again, but this time I'd record stunts I'd been jonesing to do for years. It would be called, appropriately, the Bucket List Tour. The stunts would be outrageous shit that no one had ever seen before.

Most of the ideas for the Bucket List stunts had noble beginnings. I wanted to be shot with a tranquilizer dart to raise awareness of the evils of trophy hunting. I wanted to promote spaying and neutering pets by getting a vasectomy live on camera, and then participating in a series of athletic events. I wanted to jerk off while skydiving and then ejaculate as I was in freefall to…okay, well, that one has no noble origin story whatsoever. I just thought it would be funny. Anyway, some of the stunts morphed a bit over time—when I discovered tranquilizer darts are normally loaded with ketamine, a clear no-no for me in sobriety, we pivoted to me getting general anesthesia through an IV—but they all worked well, and I built a killer hour-plus show around them.

I was really jazzed on this new act and started to think that with the Bucket List I had not only a great stand-up set, but also the foundation for a killer TV show. I could see it in my head: Each episode could tell the backstory of the stunt—what inspired it, what kept me from doing it for so long, and how it finally came together—and then would finish with the stunt itself. I connected with an Emmy Award–winning producer who had worked on the A&E series *Intervention*. I figured he could bring a level of depth and thoughtfulness to the abundant craziness that I naturally provided. This TV show would be a great way to showcase the evolution I'd made as a performer, maybe even as a person. I was fucking stoked. Together, he and I put together a can't-miss package and shopped it around. And then it totally missed. Discovery, MTV, Netflix, maybe a few others, all agreed: Hard pass.

Putting yourself out there, trying really hard at something new, feeling great about it, and *still* falling on your ass can be soul-crushing. Rejection hurts. But that's the process: Fall down. Feel like shit. Get back up.

*   *   *

The first stunt I ever did for *Jackass*—the one that got me into the cast—never aired. In it, I was walking on flaming stilts while my buddy, pro skateboarder Ryan Simonetti, ollied over my head off the roof of a house and another dude unicycled through my flaming legs. Yes, there was a lot going on there. When I initially conceived of the stunt, I pitched it to Jeff Tremaine, who at the time was publishing the anarchic skateboarding magazine *Big Brother*. I loved that magazine and had already been featured in it three times, including once on the cover, for doing things like setting my hair on fire while doing a fire-breathing backflip. I was convinced that this new, more elaborate stunt could get me on the cover of the magazine again or maybe featured in one of *Big Brother*'s underground skate videos. As it happened, it got me on *Jackass*.

At the time, most of us were coming out of that skateboarding subculture. The most accomplished skater among us was

Bam Margera, and I was super jealous of him. It wasn't just his skateboarding that made me jealous; it was the way he had packaged himself as a star, even before *Jackass* came along and really made him into one. Bam wasn't the best skateboarder in the world—although he was way better than me—but he had been putting out these awesome videos with his CKY crew and he was the central figure in them. While I was going to great lengths and essentially begging other people to put me in their skate videos, Bam was running his own productions. He was an entrepreneur and a boss. I was, at best, an employee.

Skateboarding is great because it teaches you discipline. There is no way to learn new tricks without trying and failing over and over and over and over. Wiping out, fucking up—these are very much part of skateboarding's DNA. Even world-class skaters wipe out all the time. The learning process, with its attendant bumps, bruises, and bloody scrapes, is on display for everyone to see, and there's no shame in it. A good wipeout is often cheered as loudly as landing a great trick. And even though some people might be more athletically inclined, there's no substitute for putting in the work, no shortcuts for the rich and famous. You've got to be willing to bust ass to get good.

I mention all this because I have a lot of regret over the way I basically quit on skateboarding. I mean, I always chalked it up to seeing the writing on the wall, recognizing that I would never be as good as Tony Hawk or Danny Way or even Ryan Simonetti or Bam, and then pivoting: *If I can't be a skateboarder, I can be the asshole in the skate videos who does everything but skate.* The fact that pathway worked out great for me doesn't make it any more of a bitch move that I threw in the towel on skateboarding. I figured if I couldn't measure up to Bam or Ryan or whoever, then what was the fucking point?

But here's the thing: Comparing yourself to other people is always dangerous. We're all on our own paths, our own timelines. The only way to measure your progress is to compare yourself to where you were yesterday. It's true that no matter how hard I tried, I never would've been Tony Hawk or Rob Dyrdek or Bam Margera, but that's the whole fucking point. I don't know what I would've been because I simply stopped trying to figure it out. Quitting was easier.

I thought a lot about that time in my life when I started doing stand-up. In the early days, I wasn't very good. I could've looked at Dane Cook or Sarah Silverman or Joe Rogan or Whitney Cummings and simply said, "Fuck it, I'll never be as good as them. Why waste my time?" And the thing is *I will never be as good as them*. Not because they're smarter or funnier or because they've been doing it longer than I have, but because *I am not them*. I never will be. I had to find my own path, my own unique style onstage. And because I allowed myself the time to do it, because I only compared myself to my former self, I've done just that.

*   *   *

Stand-up is just one iron I've put in the fire. I spent the first part of my life with such a narrow, single-minded approach to my career—I was going to make it as a lunatic stuntman or I was going to die trying—but this second part of my life, I've really worked on diversifying. Beyond the stand-up, there's my podcast—I know everyone and their mother has a podcast, but

I swear, mine is *really* good—there's my burgeoning career as a wildly subpar tattoo artist, and then there's a warehouse and fulfillment center that I've started operating.

If that last one seems particularly surprising and maybe a little off-brand, know that it got started from my frenzied efforts to sell loads of shit with my dumb, grinning face on it. Actually, let me give credit where it's due: My efforts to sell shit with my dumb, grinning face on it were piddling and minor league. It's when my buddy Scott Randolph started joining me on tour as a sober buddy/professional cock-blocker and saw how piddling and minor league my efforts were that things began to change. He took one look at my merch operation, which at that point consisted of me trying to sell my first book and a single T-shirt, and was incredulous.

"This is all you've got?" he asked. It was. I didn't even have a credit card reader at the time. He took it upon himself to completely transform my merch. Within a few months, after shows, he was regularly turning comedy clubs into fucking flea markets, filled with a wonderfully obnoxious amount of Steve-O branded items. These days, I sell sunglasses, posters, hats, shirts, hoodies, books, mugshot mugs, shot glasses, firecracker-up-the-butt socks, skateboard decks, and my own hot sauce. Even my dog Wendy has her own line of merch.

Scott revamped my online merch store too, and that's where the warehouse and fulfillment center came into play. Rather than outsource that stuff, Scott helped work it out so I could handle all that myself through my new company Tight Box Packing. Not only that, I'm now set up to help other people with their shipping and fulfillment operations, and I've started doing so. I think about this stuff as not just a sideline but as another potential path out of having to spend my later years doing increasingly painful shit in front of a camera for money. Although, as you know, I kind of love doing increasingly painful shit in front of a camera for money.

Look, some of these grand plans may one day fizzle into nothing, but all my eggs are no longer in the same basket, waiting to be painfully cracked. Which brings me to my last brutally insightful point: Some of the changes you implement in your life *will not work.* They are all a risk. Maybe the world doesn't want to watch your subtle period drama with Dame Judi Dench. Maybe you're actually no good at being a pastry chef. Maybe you're too old to start a career as a professional figure skater. Maybe the woman you divorced your wife for and moved across the country to be with legit can't stand you. Maybe it turns out you can't stand her either. That all sucks, but that's the process. You fall down. You feel like shit. You get back up. You try something else.

If you've been reading this chapter thinking, *Okay, Steve, that's all really interesting, but I'm not a skateboarder, a stand-up comic, or a professional stunt performer. I run the accounts payable department at a midsize marketing firm. What does this have to do with my life?* Well, first off, why does everything have to be about *you*? Oh, right, this is supposed to be a self-help book. But if I'm being serious, I don't think my big takeaways here really have anything to do with the thoroughly odd career path that I've taken. It's more about having a willingness to zig and zag on your own journey as you see fit. No one's path forward is ever a straight line. If you're in a job or a relationship that feels stifling, you can't let familiarity and comfort keep you from breaking out of it. You need to accept that whenever you embark on something new, failure is going to be a big part of your experience. If you let it derail you, you're going to be stuck exactly where you are for a long time. If you get caught up comparing where your life is right now with the lives of your buddies from high school or your ex-boyfriend or that dude you used to wait tables with at Ruby Tuesday, you're going to miss the progress you're making. And if all this seems like rather fucking obvious advice from an out-of-touch celebrity, well, what exactly did you think you were going to get when you bought this book? Besides, if it was so obvious, why haven't you done it yet?

6

Be Your Own Harshest Critic.
Then Cut Yourself a Break.

Drugs and alcohol did not make me into a first-rate fucking asshole—I could do that all by myself—but they sure as shit encouraged my worst instincts. So much of my first book was a recounting of the ways I'd been an asshole when I was loaded, but getting sober didn't exactly solve the problem. What makes that so hard to admit is that I used to have a built-in excuse. When I was loaded, you could look at my worst behavior and see a truly sick guy who you might have felt bad for. It was even oddly entertaining at times. Well, as long as you weren't the target of my wrath.

During my darkest years, I lived in an apartment complex in West Hollywood and spent an inordinate amount of time mercilessly tormenting my neighbor. I pounded a hole through the wall between our apartments, I cursed him out, I threatened him. I was angry at him for all sorts of bullshit reasons, but, in fact, he did nothing to deserve any of it. I was just being a dick because I could. Throughout that period of my life, I treated lots of people like shit and was often an arrogant, self-involved douchebag. And there are hours upon hours of video evidence out there to attest to this. I constantly had people recording every dickhead move I made, because I thought I was solidifying my legacy as some sort of supercool historical figure. It is impossible for me to watch that stuff or even think about the guy I was and not feel metric tons of embarrassment and regret.

But guess what? That's what I'm *supposed* to feel. I actually take the fact that I'm so embarrassed by that old me now as a blessing. Someone I respect a lot once told me that shame is unhealthy but regret is extremely valuable. Feeling utterly humiliated by all the extensive evidence of what an unbridled douche I can be helps to prevent me from acting like such an unbridled douche. *Most of the time.* I've gotten a lot better, but, man, I can still do some unlikable-ass shit. The one thing I have going for me now is that when I fuck up, I'm reasonably quick to acknowledge it.

We have all done things that we wish we hadn't. We have all probably had times in our lives when we weren't our best selves. Some of us manage to spend our whole lives being consistently selfish, mean-spirited, ignorant, uninformed, shallow, and unreflective, without ever realizing it or perhaps just not caring. I mean, I've got news for you: If you don't look back on who you were when you were younger and cringe about what an asshole you were, there's a distinct possibility that you're *still* an asshole.

Then again, maybe this doesn't apply to you. Maybe you have always been measured and thoughtful. Maybe you were raised by loving, well-adjusted parents to understand and practice the virtues of generosity, humility, and kindness. Maybe you have

It cost me about $8,000 to rent this billboard in Hollywood to promote my *Gnarly* comedy special. Maybe I'm nuts, but I wouldn't be surprised if I set a world record for getting the most value out of $8,000 spent on a billboard by duct-taping myself to that thing. It may have been my most effective publicity stunt ever, and I cannot believe I didn't get arrested for it. Not even a ticket! *Top photograph by Will Fox*

May 2021

SUN	MON	TUE	WED	THU	FRI	SAT
25 Scott in Hawaii / Camping TBP / TOAP 7:30pm	W18 26 Scott's Bday	27 DO A KICKFLIP 11am / 6pm Speak for Jay 6pm	28 TBP / Paul 9:30am	+3 29 Casey Niestat 10am	+1 30 Sneaker Shopping 10am / Jackass 4pm	+1 1 Jack 2pm / Rugby w Randy 4pm
2 The D.O.C. 1pm / Haircut 3pm / Action Bronson 5pm	W19 3 Shark week	4	5	6 DOC 10am	7	8
9 Shark week	W20 10 Berries 12pm / 7ates 3:30pm / Don Brown 4pm	11 TBP 12pm / Paul 12pm / D.O.C. 2pm	+1 12 Jack 11am / Nico's 7:45pm	13 Tony Hawk 2 9:45am / Action Bronson 10am	+4 14 Paul 9am / Vaccine 10:30am / Jay Leno's Garage 12pm	+1 15 UFC 262 3pm
16 Carlsbad	W21 17 Sign boards 10am / I'm Fat 10am	+2 18 LUX BDAY / Paul 11am / Green Screen! 12pm	+2 19 Paul 11am / Jack 11:10am / Green Screen! 11:30am	+3 20 Post Malone 10am / J4 Prep 11am / Jack 11am	+2 21 Paul/Jack 11am / Armando 1pm / George 2pm	+1 22 Lux in Mexico / Bike shop 12pm / UFC Garbrandt/Fonpm
23 Lux in Mexico / DAD IN LA!!! / Sign shit! 3pm	+1 24 Schwab Call 10am	+4 25 Paul 11am	+2 26 Paul 11am / Big Mouth 11:30am	+3 27 Tony Hawk 2 11am / Artie call 10am	+5 28 TBP w Dad / Troy Conrad Inkec 12pm	+2 29 Skylar Stone 6pm
30 Paul 11am / DAD IN LA!!! / Hwood 7pm	W23 31 Armando call 12pm / Inked Photo Shoot 4pm / Clean House 6pm	+1 Lima call 10:15am / Green Screen 11am / Paul/Jack 11am	+5 2 Fail Pitch NBCU 11am / Paul 11am / Next Bite Call 12pm	+2 3 GSP 10am / Fail Pitch Netflix 10:15am / Neighbor War 11am	+2 4 Paul/Jack 11am / Fail Pitch 12pm / DRAPES 12pm	+2 5 TV Destruction 10am / OA Zoom 10am / UFC Rozenstruik/S 5pm

June 2021

SUN	MON	TUE	WED	THU	FRI	SAT
30 DAD IN LA!!! / Paul 11am / Hwood 7pm	W23 31 Armando call 12pm / Inked Photo Shoot 4pm / Clean House 6pm	+1 Lima call 10:15am / Green Screen 11am / Paul/Jack 11am / We Work Meetir 11:15am	+4 2 Fail Pitch NBCU 11am / Paul 11am / Next Bite Call 12pm / Armando 1pm	+1 3 GSP 10am / Fail Pitch Netflix 10:15am / Neighbor War 11am / Paul/Jack 11am	+1 4 Paul/Jack 11am / Fail Pitch 12pm / DRAPES 12pm / Trademark Call 1pm	+1 5 TV Destruction 6am / OA Zoom 10am / UFC Rozenstruik/S 5pm
6 Paul 11am / Pasha OA 12pm / Bark Park 1:30pm	W24 7 Covid Test 10:45am / Paul 11am / Danny Trejo 2:45pm / Fail 3pm	+1 8 Athena sex toy 10:30am / Paul 11am / We Work Meetir 11:15am / Howie Mandel 2:30pm	+2 9 Shark Week 11:30am	10 T Pain 11:30am / Real Estate Call 11am / DRAPES! 12pm / Fail Pitch CW 12:30pm	+2 11 ARIZONA!!! 10am / Adam Carolla 12pm	12 UFC 263 Adesanya 8pm
13 ARIZONA!!! / Suga Sean Pod 10:45am	W25 14 Dyllan in LA / Covid Test 10:30am / Paul 11am / Jackass 4.5 cree 11:15am	+1 15 Pubes Vlog 6am / FA/Berrics 4:30pm	16 4.5 Open 9:15am / Paul 11am / TBP w Dyllan	+3 17 Dad 11am / Sign Boards! 11am	+4 18 Covid Test 10:30am / Harry's Onboarc 11:30am	+4 19 Paul 11am / Zach 2pm / Massage 8pm
20 Dyllan in LA / Rory NC	W26 21 Manscaped call 1pm	22 Dyllan/Jackass 6am / Jack 3pm	23 Paul 11am / Chris Jericho 3pm / Photo dude 6:30pm / Nico's 7:45pm	24 Duncan Trussell 11am / Studio 71 call 11am / Paul 11am / Dog Communicate 12pm	+2 25 Covid Test 11am / MeUndies 11am / Magic Spoon 12pm / Kast– Viall Files 1pm	+1 26 Paul Gone / Colombia Stem Cells
27 Paul Gone / Colombia Stem Cells	W27 28	29 Dad Vlog 6am	30 Renegade 11:30am	1 Chanel West Coas 10am / Pre-Interview Sh 11:30am	+2 2	3

July 2021

SUN	MON	TUE	WED	THU	FRI	SAT
27 Paul Gone / Colombia Stem Cells	W27 28	29 Dad Vlog 6am	30 Renegade 11:30am	1 Chanel West Coas 10am / Pre-Interview Sh 11:30am	+2 2	3
4 Paul Gone	W28 5 Covid 10am / Jack 11am / Hair cut 12pm	+2 6 Covid for ADR 10am / RZA 12pm / Fail Pitch FOX 2pm	+1 7 TBP/Smart Car / Daily Beast 12:30pm	8 SteveWillDolt 6am / Poo Cannon 7am	+1 9 UFC McGregor/Poirier 3 / J4 ADR 8am	10
11 Paul Gone / UFC McGregor/Poirier / Shark Week	W29 12 Tremaine/Knox/Ja 5pm	13 Ear Specialist 9:15am / Paul/Jack 10am / UFC Extra Rounds 2pm / Jodie Sweetin 4pm	+1 14 Paul/Jack 10am / Kyle Nelk 10:30am / Covid Test 11am / Carmax 11:30am	+3 15 Danny Trejo 6am / Paul/Jack 11am / J4 Green Screen 11am / Trump/UFC 2pm	+1 16 Elia 10am / Tredless 11:30am / Jet Suite 12pm / Peisner 6pm	+1 17 Dry Wall 10am / Mando 12pm / UFC Islam 12pm
18 TBP / Speak for Todd S 9:30am / Covid Test 12pm	W30 19 Paul 11am / Jackass Zoom 2pm / Sheckler's 8pm	20 Jackass trailer 9am / David Dobrik 11am / Raen call 1pm / Nico 7:45pm	21 NextBites 10am / Paul 12pm / Spencer X 3pm	22 Chris Jericho 6am / Trevar 11am / Paul 12:30pm	23 Trae The Truth	24 Paul 7am / UFC Dillishaw/San 1pm
25 Trae The Truth 7am	W31 26 UFC 8 Questions 10am / Covid Test 11am / Calta Lunch 12pm / Paul 3pm	+1 27 House Ear 9:20am / 10 Jackass Bits 11am / Dr. Edelstein 1pm / Paul/Jack/Cordell 1pm	+1 28 TBP / Jackass EPK 10:30am / Paul 11am / Nico's 7:45pm	29 RZA 6am	30 OKC radio 7am / Nordlinger Call 11am / Paul 11:5am / Mapilga 2pm	+1 31 Bricktown CC, OK City / Olive Tailwashers 11am / UFC Hall/Stricklanc 2pm

A snapshot of my color-coded calendar during the pandemic in 2021. The blue is for stuff that I consider a pain in the ass, and I'm slightly embarrassed to admit that Lux's birthday is shaded blue, along with everyone else's birthdays. That's no slight against Lux—or anyone else. I just fucking hate birthdays.

Climbing this highway sign near San Diego in 2014 to protest SeaWorld was harder than it looked, until I went and got a ladder! Afterwards, the Highway Patrol wanted me brought up on some fairly serious charges, but in the end, I was basically given the equivalent of a traffic ticket. Maybe the best $200 I ever spent! *Photograph by Tommy Caudill*

For eleven years, I spent the majority of my time in a never-ending cycle of airports, hotels, and comedy clubs. Not everyone was rooting for me to do well in the comedy club grind, but I couldn't be more grateful that I never gave up on putting in the work. Here I am at the Hollywood Improv in 2015. *Photograph by Olav Stubberud*

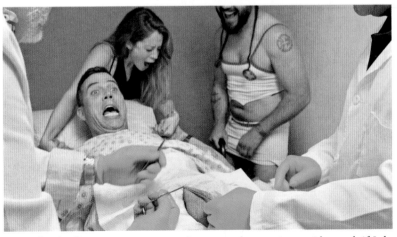

I must be the first person to ever make a comedy vasectomy video and, if I do say so myself, it is absolutely hilarious. Initially, I was worried the footage of the actual procedure wasn't shocking enough, but when I brought it on tour and screened it in theaters and comedy clubs, it became a fairly common occurrence for full-grown men to pass out upon seeing it.

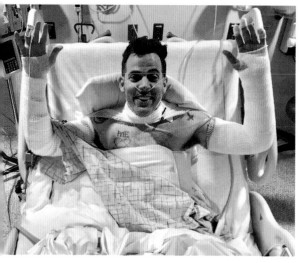

"What was your most painful stunt? This question used to really annoy me because I didn't have a definitive answer, because there are different criteria to evaluate it, including intensity and duration. Here I am in burn unit in Denver in 2017 after my buddies helped me solve that problem by igniting a bed of rocket fuel I was lying in. I'd just had skin graft surgery to deal with third-degree burns on fifteen percent of my body, which definitively checked all the boxes for the most horrific pain I've ever been in. *Photograph by Lux Wright*

I've kept track of my time spent meditating since December 27, 2019, using an app on my phone called Center. I haven't missed a single day and maintained an average of over forty minutes of meditation per day the whole time. Everything in moderation! Ha!

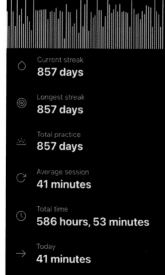

Current streak
857 days

Longest streak
857 days

Total practice
857 days

Average session
41 minutes

Total time
586 hours, 53 minutes

Today
41 minutes

For multiple Jackass films, I pitched the idea of having Mike Tyson bite a chunk out of my ear. This photo, which we took together in 2020, is the closest I ever got to making that dream a reality.

Despite the fact that I'm terrible surfing, I've traveled the world extensively to collect photos of me doing it, for what I call my "surf passport." This was what I deemed to be the best still image of me surfing in Madagascar in 2016, captured by Scott Randolph with a drone.

As I've aged, I've found my bones breaking more easily. Here, jumping on my skateboard from a wooden port-a-potty as it got wrecked by a car, I shattered my ankle, requiring a metal plate and eleven screws to put it back together. *Photograph by Jason Estudillo*

While filming *Jackass Forever*, I broke my collarbone and underwent surgery to put it back together with two plates and a bunch of screws, then I had my eyebrows ripped off by a bird of prey. Pulling out my partial denture after that made for a hell of a selfie!

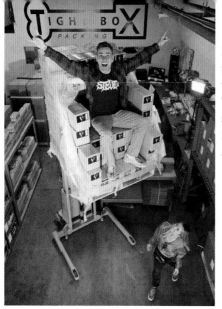

My fiancée, Lux, is a designer and styled the shoot for the cover of this book, as well as this epic throne on a forklift. Those are Tight Boxes of my own hot sauce, "Steve-O's Hot Sauce for Your Butthole," which moves a lot of units on Amazon. *Photograph by Will Fox*

Moments after I asked Lux to marry me at the taping of my *Gnarly* comedy special in 2018, Scott Randolph snapped this candid photo of us kissing. That was such an amazing night.... *Photograph by Scott Randolph*

Me getting choked unconscious by former UFC champ Chuck Liddell, while filming *Ultimate Expedition* in the Peruvian Andes in 2017.

For years, I resisted the idea of starting my own podcast, because it seemed everyone in the world had one. As in many cases, though, my right-hand man in all things, Scott Randolph, was persistent in encouraging me to do it, and it proved to be one of the best moves I ever made. Scott is also the cohost of my *Wild Ride!* podcast, and he took this photo of me with Post Malone after we interviewed him for episode number 57.

After performing in comedy clubs for eleven years straight, my experience with being on a theater tour while traveling on a tour bus has been heavenly. I seriously fuckin' love it. *Photograph by Paul Brisske*

After finding it really, really expensive to rent a tour bus I decided it would be more cost-effective to buy a huge RV and try to pass it off as a actual tour bus by getting it wrapped with my obnoxious tour art. It's a wonder that I' made it to all of my shows, because everything on this goddamn piece of shit RV is constantly failing. But even its worst days, I still love it!

I've come to really hate airports and hotels, but they are much more tolerable when I'm with the two most important females in my life . . . Lux and Wendy (our dog from the streets of Peru).

As I've grown older, it's become increasingly important to me to make better business decisions, and perhaps even more importa to come up with funny names for my businesses. I'm especially tickled by the name I came up with for my fulfillment center, which ships all of the orders for my online merch store, as well a for some third-party clients. The business has gone well enough fe me to add a second warehouse, and a fun new LED sign which I posing under here. *Photograph f Will Fox*

always been a decent human being. Lucky you. But the rest of us have our struggles with tendencies to be real fuckfaces.

What's worse is that many of us put a lot of work into defending our fuckface past selves, the stupid things we've said and done, the regrettable things we've tweeted, the bad advice we've given, the dumb business decisions we've made. Isn't it just easier to own up to things we aren't proud of, if only to establish some separation between who we really are and the unfortunate things we've occasionally done? And isn't it better to try to make them right?

*   *   *

During my out-of-control drug years, I had a manager named Nick Dunlap. I wrote about him quite a bit in my first book, and much of it was not very complimentary. When I met him, he was a rave promoter and open about the fact that his goal in life, above all else, was to make a lot of money. I think we connected because we had the same shameless attitude toward boosting my career: Anything goes. Reckless stunts, antisocial behavior, drug binges, arrests—that was all just a typical week for me during the Dunlap years. Together, we really embraced the maxim "There is no such thing as *bad* publicity." We traveled the world together for a few years, but not surprisingly, it all ended quite badly. Most of the details of the mess it became are in my first book, but suffice to say, by the time that book came out, we were not on speaking terms, there had been a lawsuit, and I carried a whole lot of resentment toward him.

A few years ago, I ran into Dunlap at a convention of YouTube creators. Fortunately, I'd grown enough to be able to see the part I'd played in the disintegration of our relationship. During the years he managed me, I was a world-class pain in the ass. Frankly, he was a trouper (if not a saint) for putting up with me back then. When I saw him, I went up to him, and we spoke casually about what we'd been up to for the last fifteen or so years; then I asked if he was doing anything for dinner. We went and sat on the patio of a nearby restaurant, and I spilled what I had to say. I owned up to being a real piece of shit back when we'd worked together. I addressed the differences that we had: Beyond the legal issues, I had said some things about him that I really regret. That was some extra shit, and it sucked dick. He told me that it meant a lot to him to hear that and quickly acknowledged his role in it all. We're not best buddies now—we're not really even in touch—but that helped me let go of any negativity between me and him, and also helped me acknowledge to myself the ways that I've changed and grown since then.

I'm a big believer in being your own harshest critic, and doing that in the presence of a former antagonist. It's a great way to open a dialogue with someone, heal old wounds, and maybe even rebuild a bridge that had been burned. It's also a great way of demonstrating that you are not the same person who torched that bridge in the first place.

*   *   *

Not long ago, I had Violent J from the Insane Clown Posse on my podcast. Part of the reason I wanted him on was because I'd been such a prick to him back in the day. Around 2004, I was on tour in Orlando, with the aforementioned Nick Dunlap and one of the *Jackass* guys. I can't remember which *Jackass* guy was on that leg, though I definitely recall that Dave England had recently quit the tour because he could no longer stand to be around me. He was replaced by a twelve-foot king cobra that this lunatic snake expert named David Weathers would release onstage and then kiss on the head. I don't know what the hell we were thinking with that. If this guy had gotten bitten by the snake—which was not defanged or de-venomized in any way—there would've been nobody capable of corralling it to prevent it from literally killing anyone else in the venue. As I understand it, that snake could've taken down an elephant, but I didn't think much about consequences back then.

The shows I was doing were really just hard-core mayhem: I'd do some tricks and stunts—balance furniture on my chin, set myself on fire, staple my nut sack to my leg, chew glass—but what people got really excited about was coming onto the stage to do dumb shit themselves. I'd invite volunteers from the crowd to get kicked in the nuts, I'd allow audience members to drink cups full of my urine, I'd line guys up and have contests to see who could give themselves a black eye first. By the end of the show, the stage would be a mess of alcohol, blood, piss, and vomit. All the while, I'd incessantly behave like a belligerent, entitled shithead, both onstage and off. I mean, Dunlap was paying the *Jackass* guys thousands of dollars to come on tour with me, and even that wouldn't keep them from quitting. That's how much fun I was to be around.

I bumped into Violent J at the hotel in Orlando before my show. The Insane Clown Posse—who, if you don't know them, are a horrorcore-rap duo who dress up like clowns and have an intensely rabid cult fan base who call themselves Juggalos—had a concert in town but were off that day. J was incredibly nice to me, told me he was a big fan, and at first, I think I was tolerable to him. He came and hung out in my hotel room, and even gave me this pretty dope ICP jersey, but pretty quickly I started giving him shit. In between snorting rails of coke, I told him that I was a graduate of the Ringling Bros. and Barnum & Bailey Clown College (which was true), and that the Insane Clown Posse were not *real* clowns. I told him he was putting his greasepaint on wrong. I made fun of his music. I was just being disrespectful. And the whole time, I had cameramen filming this interaction.

Later, he came to my show, and I made a point of inviting him onstage. He'd already told me he doesn't go onstage without his clown makeup on, so he wouldn't come up. That was my cue to start calling him a pussy and just trashing him. I was such a dick. He would've been completely justified in kicking my ass, and I know he thought about it, but ultimately he never bothered to. In fact, it was so common for me to act that way that I'd largely forgotten about the incident until I saw him on a YouTube video talking about his beef with me. Then it all came flooding back.

When we spoke on my podcast, I started off by recognizing what a colossal douche I had been to him. What happened next is what usually happens, at least with many people who are worth building a relationship with: He was completely gracious about it. We were able to move on, and soon after he invited me to host the main stage at ICP's legendary music festival, the Gathering of the Juggalos. I'm proud to now call him a friend.

Making amends isn't simply a chore to be crossed off a list, and it's not always going to go well. Of course, you hope these interactions make other people feel better and maybe even repair some relationships, but that's not really the point. Whether or not the people I've wronged have appreciated my attempts to make things right—that old neighbor of mine certainly had no interest in ever speaking to me when I reached out to him in sobriety—the point is to hold myself accountable for the person I have been (and sometimes continue to be). When I acknowledge what an asshole I've been, I increase the odds of avoiding being that asshole again.

* * *

As I mentioned before, 2013 was a rough year for me. My career felt like it was in the dumps, so in an effort to drum up some new opportunities for myself I took a meeting with someone who wanted to be my manager. He walked in and practically the first thing he said was "It's all about the digital space now." He told me that I needed to have my own YouTube channel, I needed to start a podcast, I needed to be posting all kinds of new content to my social media accounts regularly.

What I heard was: *You need to work your ass off by yourself for free and then I'll take ten percent of your income.*

So, fuck that guy, right? What was he bringing to the table? Even if he was right, why would I need him to do any of this shit anyway? He wasn't proposing that he lift a finger to help me produce any of that content. The whole meeting felt like a transparent grab at taking a piece of my touring revenue, which at the time was pretty much all my revenue. What did this asshole know anyway? I might not have been actually working on shit (unless you consider schlepping back and forth to comedy clubs around the country "working on shit"), but I was a TV star, dammit! I'd been in the number one movie in the country multiple times! And he wanted me to act like posting shit on social media constituted an actual career? That sounded like a terrible and embarrassing demotion.

Not too long after that meeting, I got a call from an old writer-director friend of mine named Sam Macaroni. Back in the bad old days, Sam was one of my chief partners in crime. We used to party so much together that when I finally got sober, I knew for sure I couldn't be hanging out with him. But when Macaroni called me in 2013, he told me straight off the bat that he had been sober for six months. He'd held off on reaching out before then because he wanted me to know he was serious about it.

When we met up later that week, Macaroni told me that he had been making a great living the past couple of years creating content for YouTube. "You gotta get on YouTube!" he told me. "You will kill on there."

First that manager dude and now my old buddy Sam? Who would be the next person to suggest that I start slumming it on social media like a loser who's trying to make it big? I already had made it big! Why would I want to take such an embarrassing step backward? But Macaroni insisted I give it a try and promised to help me out. He had this infectious enthusiasm, and I'd really missed him a lot. Besides, I didn't have a hell of a lot else to do at that moment, so what the fuck?

Not too long after that, he filmed the first video I'd make specifically for YouTube, a hidden-camera video where I walked around and unfurled a used condom loaded with (fake) splooge upon unsuspecting people who wanted to take selfies with me. More important, he took the time to teach me how to edit it. Every time I called him with a question, he picked up the phone. I'd been obsessed with collecting video footage of myself since I was a teenager, so it's almost shocking that in all that time I'd never learned how to properly edit the footage on a computer or even shown much of an interest in learning. In my head, I was the talent, and the talent *was* the content; it didn't sit crouched over a computer in a dark room editing.

But as I was learning, the reality of the entertainment business is different now. That line between *in front of the camera* and *behind the camera* has been obliterated. The entire paradigm has shifted. I'd been looking at YouTube—or any social media platform—as a step down from the heights of TV and movie stardom. But the fact is, YouTube was a way to take control of my career. I'd been banging my head against the wall, begging industry executives to get behind my ideas and make them happen. They all kept rejecting me. It turned out I didn't need them anyway. Nothing was stopping me from filming my own ideas, editing the videos myself, and building an audience to share them with. At the time, I wasn't even looking at YouTube as a path to any sort of financial success. The creative freedom that came with my newfound ability to produce my own content kept me sane during that otherwise incredibly dark year.

The truth is, going back to my teenage years, I never viewed my video footage as a way to make money. It was always about just getting people to see the shit I was doing and the footage I'd collected. Since fifteen, I'd been corralling whomever I could wherever I could—in dorm rooms, in restaurants, in garages—to watch my latest shitty VHS cassette recording of me skateboarding or scaling an apartment building or doing backflips while blowing fireballs. I desperately needed the validation of others, whether it was a room full of friends, or a cable TV network, or a movie studio, to tell me that what I was doing was worth watching. (Hell, I still do!) But all these social media platforms were just easier access to bigger rooms with more people in them. Posting my stuff on YouTube and Instagram wasn't a humbling admission of career failure, it was an acknowledgment that the world is changing and that I had to adapt.

Once I shook off my middle-aged thinking and went all in on social media, it completely revamped my career. Anytime I have an idea, I can film it, edit it, and know that it will be seen by millions of people—almost certainly more than have seen just about anything I've done on TV in the past decade. All this has given me a direct connection to my fans and made me the only executive I need approval from. There's no one telling me what to do or that we don't have enough money to do some stunt or that it's not going to hit with the demographic that advertisers are aiming for. It's just me. And I owe Sam Macaroni a great debt for how he helped me realize all this. And I may even owe something to that manager whom I dismissed out of hand back in 2013. Though definitely not ten percent.

The big takeaway from all this, though, is not about YouTube or sobriety or the universal appeal of draping a used condom over a stranger's shoulder, but rather about not getting stuck in old patterns that no longer serve you. Sometimes it makes sense to interrogate your most cherished beliefs. To open your mind to the possibility that it's time to make some changes. It's okay to admit you were wrong. In fact, I think it's a hell of a lot better than pretending you weren't and continuing to *be* wrong.

Strangely, the world today often doesn't look that kindly on this type of evolution. We've become a culture that is slightly obsessed with nailing people to the wall for their worst decisions without allowing for the possibility that people can and do change. This isn't to say we shouldn't hold people accountable for their actions or that we should ignore the past, but if I was judged simply by the worst things I've done, I'd be fucked. I've done a lot of bad things.

I see this manifest itself in the tattoos I've gotten and later altered or removed when I realized what a terrible idea they were. Tattoos are funny, because most people see them as a literal imprinting onto your skin of your core ideals or things that are important to you. Me, I've gotten most of my tattoos because they made me laugh. Of course, what I think is funny changes over time, so my tattoos occasionally have too. I used to have "S-H-I-T" and "F-U-C-K" tattooed on my knuckles, but I got them lasered off. Actually, I still think those were pretty funny, but, man, having that stuff tattooed on my hands was an overly aggressive statement to most everyone I encountered, and at a point, it became a statement I no longer felt compelled to make.

Back in 2006, I was getting drunk with some buddies, talking about how I never wanted to have kids. I decided to get a tattoo memorializing this opposition to procreating. At first I was going to get a picture of a baby with a red line going through it, *Ghostbusters* style, meaning, "No babies." As I got drunker, that morphed into getting the phrase "Fuck Babies" tattooed onto my skin. Somehow, by the time I got to the tattoo parlor, I was drunk enough to tell the tattoo artist to ink a drawing of a guy fucking a baby onto my arm. As soon as I walked out onto the street and showed people that tattoo, even the very drunken version of me knew I had made a colossal mistake. People were justifiably horrified. I quickly got that tattoo covered up by turning the baby into an ostrich, which doesn't make much sense, but was objectively funny to look at and inspired an old joke of mine: When your *cover-up* tattoo is a man fucking an ostrich, you know you started off with something bad.

I still catch shit for that tattoo when people find out about it, and I totally get why, but for the most part, I'm okay with my tattoos being something of a road map of awful decisions. Some of them are truly offensive, but at some point I thought they were a good enough idea to get them etched into my skin. So, in that way, they're a very tangible reminder of the guy I used to be.

We think of tattoos as being so permanent, but with the advent of tattoo removal technology, they're potentially far less permanent than whatever dumbass shit we've posted on Instagram, Facebook, TikTok, or Twitter. With everyone leaving this lasting digital record of most everything they do, increasingly there is going to be evidence of the person you used to be out in the world anyway. So doesn't it make sense to acknowledge that that person existed, make peace with the ways in which he sucked, and then congratulate yourself on not being him anymore?

7

Health 101: You Only Get
One Body So Don't Fuck It Up
(Too Badly)

I know the title of this chapter is pretty fucking rich coming from a guy who has literally made a living fucking up his body, but the truth is, I'm actually not as fucked up as you might think. Once I got sober, I started taking stock of the damage I'd done to myself with drinking, drugs, and the assorted lunacy I'd engaged in both personally and professionally. I visited various doctors and medical professionals, who, on the whole, were relatively astonished to discover that I was in reasonable, functioning condition. Which is not the same as saying I have no problems whatsoever.

As I mentioned a few chapters ago, as you get older, your body doesn't bend as much without breaking. After shattering my ankle doing that skateboarding stunt with Danny Way and snapping my collarbone trying to wakeboard behind a horse for *Jackass Forever*, it took quite a lot of screws to put me back together, but as painful as both those things were, I avoided anything stronger than Tylenol and Advil to manage the pain. Although I feel like my sobriety has been solid, I know myself well enough to understand that I can't be trusted around painkillers.

That became an issue when I set myself on fire doing snow angels in flaming rocket fuel on my living room floor (as one does). I had serious burns and these gnarly boils all over my arms after that stunt, but I thought I'd be okay. I'd been burned lots of times before and usually just kind of gritted my way through it. But each day after that incident was even more unbearable than the day before. My skin was peeling off in sheets, and the pain was intense. At the time, I had comedy dates booked in Denver, so I flew there, where I did a show on Thursday and two on Friday. But by Saturday, I couldn't take it anymore, so I finally went to a hospital.

I want to take a second here to talk a little about pain and enduring it. Because I've spent most of my life hurting myself for the amusement of others, people always assume I have a high tolerance for pain. If anything, the opposite is true. The very fact that you can see how much pain I'm in when I'm doing a stunt is part of the appeal. It's not really that interesting to watch some dude get electrocuted if he can just grin and bear it. I don't grin and bear much of anything.

For years, people would always ask me, "What's the most painful stunt you've ever done?" I always found that question frustrating, because I never had a satisfying answer. There are two basic parts to calculating pain: How much does it hurt? And how long does it hurt? Getting shocked with a cattle prod is acute and incredibly painful, but it's over quickly. If I wipe out on my bike and scrape up my ass on the pavement, it doesn't hurt that badly in the moment, but the hurt tends to stick around for a long time, because it's complicated by sitting down, standing up, and having to peel your boxers off your butt cheeks. Well, these rocket fuel burns fell into both categories—they hurt like fucking hell and they didn't quit. The only upside was that I finally had a good answer for that question about which stunt hurt the most.

At the hospital, they sent me straight to the burn unit, where the doctor told me they'd need to rush me in for emergency skin graft surgery—essentially, they'd somehow cut off the burns and then cover the patches with skin from cadavers, which actually sounded pretty rad. They could see that I was in excruciating pain and were prepared to give me Dilaudid, a powerful opiate, to help me manage it. I refused, because I felt like it would endanger my sobriety. But then they found out that I'd just eaten before coming to the hospital, which meant they couldn't operate on me right away. I'd have to wait at least eight hours before I'd have any relief from the agony I was in. For the first time in my sober life, that was too much to bear. I agreed to the Dilaudid.

My arms were so fucked up from the burns that they had to shoot the Dilaudid into my neck, and although it helped with the pain, over the course of those eight hours, the pain returned. So I asked for more Dilaudid, which they gave me. Then I asked for more again. The nurse told me that they could give me more, but it was going to get to the point soon where getting me off the drug was going to be an issue. I was in a bit of a narcotic haze at the time, but when she told me that, it quickly cut through the fog, and the realization of what was going on hit home hard. *Oh, yeah, I'm a fucking drug addict!* I had heard many stories of sober people relapsing in this exact fashion. I immediately told her I didn't want any more Dilaudid. After the surgeries, I was given a prescription for a painkiller but never filled it.

Before I overdo it congratulating myself for bravely steering clear of painkillers and give you the impression that I'm just over here gliding through sobriety like some sort of fucking hero, let me be clear: I'm not. When I first committed myself to the path of recovery, I genuinely believed that my sobriety *would* make me some sort of fucking hero, and that it would rejuvenate my career, resulting in all sorts of cash and prizes. But that didn't happen. It's just as well, because if that had remained my motivation, I'm sure I would've relapsed long ago. Thankfully, my impetus for doing the work of recovery is, quite simply, to not be the intolerable douchebag drugs and alcohol had frequently aided me in being. Just that is enough for me to make sobriety my number one priority. Most days I do pretty well with that, but at times I have quietly slipped into some dangerous areas.

Take, for example, my rather laissez-faire attitude toward anesthesia. Some sober people call anesthesia a "free-lapse," because you can't really expect someone to let a surgeon cut them open without anesthetic. Which is certainly a fair point, but that doesn't mean that the drugs used in anesthesia aren't drugs. And at times, I've sort of disregarded that fact.

I've already mentioned my idea for a stunt that I thought would raise awareness about the evils of trophy hunting. All these people want to get photos of themselves with lions and cheetahs and whatnot. Well, what if instead of having to kill the animal, they just shot them with tranquilizer darts, took their photo, and moved on? I envisioned a stunt in which I played the animal in this scenario, got shot with a tranquilizer dart, and then tried to run as far as I could before collapsing in a heap. I thought it'd be both hilarious and instructive. We found a guy who was more than happy to shoot me, which I was thrilled about, but when the guy explained that the drug in the darts was ketamine, that was a real problem for me. Because I always fucking *loved* ketamine.

Nonetheless, I hung on to this tranquilizer dart bit for a while. The whole thing was completely misguided. At one point, we were flying to South Africa for a surf trip, and we decided to call some anti-poaching organizations there to talk to them about promoting tranquilizer darts as a safer alternative. The reaction of these organizations could accurately be summed up as "What the fuck are you assholes talking about with tranquilizer darts? We promote leaving animals the fuck alone." Because of course they do.

The idea never totally went away, though. Instead, it gradually morphed into me being knocked out by general anesthesia while hauling ass on a bicycle. We found a medical professional who was willing not only to administer this anesthetic but also to procure it from the place where they worked. Nobody needs to know where, when, or how that happened. In fact, when we filmed the stunt, nobody on the set ever saw that medical professional's face except for me and Lux. To say that tensions were high that day would be the ultimate understatement. Let's be clear: general anesthesia drugs make people stop breathing. That's why they put a tube down your throat to breathe for you during surgery. We were doing this in a grassy field in the middle of nowhere, recklessly risking the career this medical professional worked for years to attain, and, oh yeah, also my life. The professional explained that we should administer the drug into an IV in my arm incrementally, so as to "knock me out, but not stop my breathing." I agreed that that seemed like a good idea.

I suppose you could argue that approach was incredibly dangerous in other ways, because by giving it to me bit by bit, the anesthesia never managed to knock me out at all. By the time we ran out of the drug, I had been given almost three times the amount that Google had told me was generally required for a surgical procedure on a full-grown adult male. Not only was the stunt a colossal failure because I never even keeled over, but it culminated in me riding that bicycle around completely loaded on what were still drugs, even if that drug wasn't ketamine.

In the end, that stunt rattled my sobriety. I was deeply upset about it and can honestly say that it made me question whether I could really call myself sober. The good news is that I spoke up about it, both before and after, to a group of men in recovery whom I regularly lean on to get me through difficult times. The fact that I kept no secrets and that my intentions had purely been to get the footage of the stunt helped me reconcile the whole episode. Thankfully, it's now been more than three years since then, and I've had no further serious issues with maintaining my sobriety.

Also—and this is nearly as important—I'm happy to report that I found a way to salvage the bit! I won't say where, when, or how, but I met a doctor who offered to put a four-inch needle into my spinal cavity and inject a drug that would render me paralyzed from the waist down while I attempted to run as far as I could. This sort of injection is relatively localized, non-mood-altering, and doesn't affect the brain, so it never called my sobriety into question. And the footage was insane. It all just goes to show what I've been hammering on about for a while: When you fail, you've got to pick yourself up, dust yourself off, and try again to fall flat on your face.

* * *

Remember at the beginning of this chapter when I was telling you that my body is in good working condition despite all the shit I've put it through? I'll stand by that statement, but if there's one possible exception to that, you'll find it in my mouth. Well, in my mouth and down my throat.

To start with, I have something called Barrett's esophagus, which means the lining of my esophagus is eroded. This can be a precursor to esophageal cancer, so I've tried to be diligent about taking care of it, and it seems to be more under control now than it once was. It's not definitive that all the vomiting I did for years, both as a drunk and in my career—I have often described myself as a professional bulimic—caused this condition, but it damn sure did not help. Regardless, I've tried to eliminate vomiting from my arsenal of go-to bits.

Those years of puking also likely did some damage to my teeth and gums, though, to be honest, I've done so many things to fuck up my teeth and gums, it's hard to quantify what's to blame. Eating copious amounts of sugar? Check. Chewing glass? Check. A serious long-term cocaine habit? Double check. Pouring rubbing alcohol in my mouth in order to blow fireballs? I know it's hard to believe, but that is also not great for your gums. But of all the things I've done to fuck up my mouth, you want to know the thing that I'm almost positive was the worst? Not flossing.

I swear to God. Of all those stupid things I've done, all the wild, dangerous, unhealthy shit I've put my poor mouth through, the one I regret the most is not flossing. In fact, if there is one piece of serious health advice that I feel confident about giving you in this book, that's it: Floss your motherfucking teeth!

The sum total of all this damage is not minor. For years, I had gross yellow teeth and horrible breath. I was incredibly self-conscious about both. My mouth was like a bacteria farm. Even as I've finally started to deal with all this crap, it's been a long, painful road. I've been through multiple sets of fake teeth and countless grueling oral surgeries. I've had gum grafts, bone grafts, and dental implants (which didn't work because my bone loss is so bad...from not flossing!). It's been a fucking horror show. These days, my fake teeth are almost embarrassingly shiny and white. I am resigned to the fact that I will one day need dentures—perhaps one day soon—but I guess if this is the steepest price I have to pay for the shit I've put my body through, then I got off easy.

The fact is, even with all that shit I just mentioned, as I close in on fifty, I am probably no worse off than most dudes my age: a little heavier than I want to be, a little achier every morning, frequently nursing a stiff back because I don't maintain a decent stretching regimen, but otherwise still ticking.

So, how have I managed this feat? First, let's be clear, there is a significant part of your health that is not totally in your control. It's down to luck, to your genes, to the whims of fate. And that's at least part of my story. I've been really fucking lucky. And while I'm extremely grateful for that luck, there's not much I can do to explain it or pass it on to you. But I still feel it is important to acknowledge instead of feeding you some bullshit about treating my body like a holy temple. Because, really, in my life, I've done far more shit that was terrible for me than stuff that was good for me. Over the last decade, though, I've been trying hard to balance that equation.

Acknowledging the role of genes and luck is not the same as throwing up your arms and saying, "Fuck it! It's beyond my control. I'm just going to eat, drink, smoke, and do whatever the fuck I want until I drop one day." I mean, you're welcome to do that. I can't stop you. In fact, that was pretty much my philosophy before I sobered up, but back then I also thought I was going to be dead before I was thirty. So there's that. The fact is, there is plenty you can do for your health that is totally within your control. Which is not to say it's easy.

*   *   *

Growing older brings some hard truths with it. Your body becomes a much more temperamental machine as it ages. For many of us, when we're young, we can eat like feral pigs, and as long as we get off our asses a few times a day to do something more rigorous than open the refrigerator door, we still look and feel reasonably healthy. I know, for me, until I turned about thirty-three, I was always pretty slim and never really thought much about how I got that way. But since then, it feels like I'm thinking about it *all the fucking time.*

As you get older, your metabolism changes, and, quite quickly, you're heavier than you once were, you're moving slower, your muscles and joints feel stiffer. And because you've let yourself go, there are all sorts of knock-on effects: Maybe your back is killing you, your knees hurt, your blood pressure is shooting through the roof, your sex drive is going in the opposite direction, and you're depressed because, well, shit, look at yourself—you're a fucking mess! It's amazing how the problems cascade when our physical health gets compromised.

You don't need to be a board-certified physician to know that the two main things you can do to keep your body functioning well are to exercise and to control your diet. Let's start with the first of those tasks.

I know some people claim to love working out. Not me. I hate the gym. I don't jog. Any sort of repetitive exercise bores me to tears. I've always had a sneaking suspicion that most of the people who talk about how much they love working out really don't like working out either. I mean, what the fuck is there to like about doing something really hard and incredibly boring, over and over, until it hurts and you're exhausted?

I think people just like the feeling of being *done* working out. That part I get. Anytime you finish a horrible task, it feels great to know that you don't have to do it anymore. But as for the fitness freaks who genuinely enjoy putting on their Lululemon yoga pants, going to Planet Fitness, and blasting their quads, fuck those people. They can skip this part of the book.

For the rest of us normal people, we're in a bit of a bind: How do we find ways to exercise when exercising so often sucks so much? The thing that I've figured out—and you didn't need me to tell you this—is that you've got to find activities that you actually want to do, that will keep you in fighting shape, and that you can continue to do even as your body cooperates with you less and less.

I like to tell people that what I found that works for me is surfing. But the truth about me and surfing is not that simple. I mean, surfing *is* genuinely something I like to tell people about because I really like the *idea* of being a surfer. I like the gear, I like the places you go do it, I like the people who do it, I like the whole lifestyle and mystique that exists around it. If I'm being totally honest, I like all that stuff way more than I like the physical act of surfing. Because surfing itself is really fucking hard.

To explain to you how I first got into surfing I have to begin by telling you a story about me *not* surfing. The first time I ever went to Hawaii, back before I was sober, I was on one of those debauchery-filled stunt tours that guy Nick Dunlap organized. Everybody on the tour decided to go surfing one day, and I came along to the beach with them. I wasn't interested in trying to surf, though, mostly because I had a whole lot of cocaine and couldn't figure out how I could possibly concentrate on doing coke if I was floating on a surfboard in the ocean.

So, while everyone else was out surfing and having a lovely, sun-dappled afternoon, I was sitting on the beach like a fucking dirtbag, drinking beers and snorting line after line of blow. At one point, I had so much cocaine clogged up in one of my nostrils that I blew my nose and it came out in a big hard glob of cocaine and snot. Ever the resourceful drug addict, I poked holes in one of the empty beer cans, made it into a pipe, and smoked this huge glob that had come out of my nose. I called it crack boogers. That was me back then.

Fast-forward to 2012: I'm sober, and I'm in Maui on a comedy tour. We had nothing to do during the day, but I was more than content to sit in my hotel room and watch the NFL playoffs on TV. One of the comics who was opening for me knocked on the door and told me that some local guys wanted to take me surfing. I looked around at my comfy bed in my nice hotel room and had no interest in leaving. But then I thought back to my previous trip to Hawaii and the crack boogers. I felt shitty about having spent that day like that. Did I want to be able to tell people I was in Maui and I sat in my hotel room watching TV, or that I was in Maui and I went surfing? I didn't really want to do it, but I didn't want to have not done it either. So off I went.

At the beach, the waves were small, bordering on nonexistent. As I later discovered, on a day like that, any idiot can get up on a big longboard, and in this case, I was any idiot. But I wasn't content to be just that. At some point, I got the idea to try to do a headstand on the board. Even though the waves were tiny, riding a surfboard upside down, balancing on your head as that board moves along the water, is tricky. And when I pulled it off, the guy who had rented me the big, foam longboard captured a photo of me doing it, a photo which I absolutely fell in love with and cherish dearly to this very day.

That was kind of what hooked me into surfing. I liked how it made me look. I liked the *idea* of it. I liked walking with a board under my arm, or having one strapped to the side of my van. Basically, I liked that I thought it made me look cool.

I made a conscious decision to become a surfer. I had friends who were already into it, so that helped. What also helped was that most of the places to go surfing were either nearby in California or involved taking trips to exotic locales with my friends.

In fact, there is probably nothing I'm prouder of since I took up surfing than what I call my "surf passport." My surf passport is a collection of the best photos from each of these destinations: Costa Rica, El Salvador, Morocco, the Maldives, Alaska, Fiji, the Dominican Republic, the Philippines, Peru, Madagascar, Canada, Hawaii, Australia, South Africa, Nicaragua. These trips have been amazing, and they remind me a little of the time I spent with Chris Pontius traveling the world for our MTV show, *Wildboyz*. The big difference is that back then I was still getting loaded and arrived in these foreign lands most concerned with procuring weed and fast food. The sober version of me is far more appreciative of the chance to really experience these places.

It's worth mentioning that the year I kick-started my surf passport was, not at all coincidentally, the same year that I was in a deep depressive funk. I mentioned this earlier in the book: That was 2013, the year Johnny Knoxville and Jeff Tremaine were getting ready to release *Bad Grandpa*, a feature film under the *Jackass* banner but without any of the other guys from *Jackass* in it. It seemed to drill home for me just how little I had going on in my career (and my life) at the time. I think I wanted to lean into my depression by being in some far-off place, in the middle of the ocean, feeling sorry for myself. I took trips to Canada, Nicaragua, El Salvador, the Maldives, and the Dominican Republic that year, on what could fairly be called my World Pouting Tour. On some level, I was definitely just wallowing in it, but also, being out there, getting exercise in these fascinating places, usually with my buddy Tommy Caudill, who is an incredibly positive, supportive guy, made me feel better.

I fully recognize how completely ridiculous it is for me to be touting the glories of wildly expensive international travel as a reason to take up surfing. Most people won't be able to afford this kind of thing. Believe me, I'm not bringing it up to convince you to go buy an $800 surfboard and a $2,000 plane ticket to Tahiti, but rather to point out how impure and tainted my love for this sport really is. I mean, the one thing I haven't mentioned at all in this treatise on the joys of surfing is any joys whatsoever about the actual surfing.

The thing is, once I'm in the ocean with a surfboard, it's not like I become one with the waves. For me, that is where the fun stops and the agony begins. It's just really, really difficult. Surfing requires the existence of nice-size waves coming in toward the shore with force. But in order to get on those waves, you've got to paddle through that force, through what's called "the impact zone." And I suck at that. My God, do I suck at that. It's excruciating work that involves hard swimming, trying to duck dive under the waves, getting thrown off my board, hoping to God it doesn't hit someone else, and swallowing a shitload of salt water.

When I finally make it out to what's called "the lineup," it really doesn't get any better. No matter where you go in the world—and as I've told you, I've traveled far and wide, to remote corners of the Earth—there is pretty much no such thing as getting a wave to yourself. The water is usually crowded with surfers waiting in the lineup. And there is strict etiquette around that. If someone else is already on a wave, you are not allowed to "drop in" on them, because you may in fact do exactly that and drop in on top of them, causing a dangerous collision. I've gotten cursed out by many an angry surfer for breaking this cardinal rule. So you've got to wait your turn. When mine comes, it almost doesn't matter whether I get up on my board—which probably happens less than half the time on my best days—or whether I eat shit, because fifteen seconds later, I'm back in the impact zone, paddling for my life.

Look, it's genuinely exhilarating to get up and actually ride a wave, but that lasts maybe ten seconds. Some days it doesn't happen at all. More than a few of my so-called surf sessions have not technically involved me doing any surfing whatsoever, just near-drowning in the ocean for hours. Ultimately, even on the best days, the work and pain it takes me to paddle out, get in a lineup, and finally get up on the board is so wildly out of proportion to the few seconds of glory that I get while I'm actually riding a wave. I spend most of my time in the water being completely miserable. It's worth mentioning that this is not everybody's experience with surfing. It's probably not most people's. But it's mine.

So, what's my point with all this? Well, I have two. The first is that even at its very worst moments, I still would rather be out huffing and puffing, wrestling with my surfboard, than running on a treadmill or swimming laps at a local YMCA. Even when it sucks, I can tell myself, "I'm out on the ocean, it's a beautiful day, I'm getting exercise with my friends, and there's a decent chance I'm going to get ten joyous seconds of riding a wave out of this." That's something.

My second point is that I have created an architecture around this exercise activity that has made it not just doable but something I very much look forward to doing. The beach, the lifestyle, the photos, the attention, being with my buddies, traveling—these have all made the rigors of surfing worth enduring.

For most people, surfing won't be the answer. If you live nowhere near the ocean, don't have a lot of disposable income, can't swim, etc., you're going to need to find something else in your life to do regularly. Maybe it's an activity you already love, like playing basketball or hiking, or maybe, like me, it's an activity you don't much like but can figure out a way to make enjoyable. I know guys who are married with young kids who look forward to going for a run every day, not because they like running but because they know they can put in their earbuds and have forty-five minutes to themselves, listening to their favorite podcast. Another guy I know has a stationary bike and looks forward to the thirty minutes he rides it each day, because that's the time when he allows himself to binge-watch trashy TV shows. Other people I know run or work out with friends, making that time as much about socializing as exercising. It's all about making it something you want to do, because if it feels like a chore, I guarantee you will expend more energy thinking of reasons not to do it than you ever spend doing it.

*   *   *

So that's exercise totally sorted out for you. You're welcome. I will admit I am not nearly as confident dispensing advice about eating a healthy diet. Food has always been a problem for me, since I was a kid. When I was in school, I would save my lunch money so I could spend it all on candy bars and soda. And I had no sense of restraint whatsoever. I ate candy alcoholically. I'd binge on Snickers or Twix.

All that set in motion a lifetime of troublesome, over-the-top eating habits. At times, I've been a militant—and, yes, annoyingly self-righteous—vegan. At others, I've been the scourge of militant and annoyingly self-righteous vegans. I've been a vegetarian, I've been a pescetarian, I've been gluten-free, I've been dairy-free, and I've been sugar-free. In addition to all this, I have long had what I call a condiment disorder. Ketchup, mustard, mayo, hot sauce, whatever comes in a plastic container and sits on the middle of the table, I promise you, I am going to drown my goddamn food in it. However much you're thinking, it's way, way more.

These categories and habits aren't even mutually exclusive. There have been times when I'm a practicing vegan but think nothing about ordering an extra-large Impossible Whopper meal from Burger King, occasionally with an extra Impossible Whopper, and then burying it all in ketchup. Yes, technically vegan. No, not remotely healthy. I thought about writing an entire book about my eating habits, but it would almost certainly need to be shelved in the Horror section. I think the best I can offer you is to tell you the story of my food issues, which are a constant work in progress, and which at the very least will make you feel better about that late-night bowl of ice cream you've been prone to sneaking on occasion.

We all eat for many different reasons, and for me, hunger would struggle to sneak into the top ten. I have thought very deliberately about the way I eat, and I have also thought very deliberately about how thinking very deliberately about the way I eat impacts the way I eat. It's all a bit dizzying.

I first became a vegetarian back when I was still drinking

and drugging. In fact, this was during the final weeks leading up to my intervention, when I had spent so much time experiencing psychosis and all its attendant hallucinations that I felt like I was privy to a world of supernatural beings that mere mortals couldn't see. Amid all this, my reasoning for cutting meat out of my diet was kind of like a deathbed conversion. I remember seeing this video on YouTube of a Hare Krishna dude asking how you could expect to be "saved" if you were eating animals that were killed for your consumption. I was very much obsessed with the afterlife at that point in my lunacy, and I just figured since I had no good answer to that question, I better quit eating meat or I'd be fucked in my afterlife.

After I sobered up, I quickly cut out all animal products and became a vegan. As is often the case with new converts to anything, I was a zealous motherfucker. Some addicts are always looking for something to be addicted to, and without drugs and alcohol, veganism became my new addiction. I blabbed about it to anyone who would listen and many who would not.

My intentions were not bad: As a newly sober person, I needed to build my self-esteem through doing good things that made me feel good about myself. Being a vegan absolutely fell into that category. Veganism was a way for me to be compassionate and being compassionate felt rewarding. The problem with all this is that it can quickly become a self-righteous crusade. On some level, I believed that choosing to eat a veggie burger when I would've rather had an actual Whopper made me a better person than you. When I went to buy a new pillow from Target, one of my animal-rights-loving vegan friends explained that pillows made with feathers are cruel, so I got a foam one and felt like I should be a candidate for fucking sainthood.

I became something of a vegan fundamentalist for a while. In 2011, I stormed out of a fundraiser for the American Diabetes Association because they were serving meat, which some studies have shown can increase the risk of developing diabetes. As I told TMZ immediately after the incident—because who else would I tell?—it was like serving alcohol at an AA meeting. A few years later, I saw a documentary called *Cowspiracy*, which focused attention on the meat and dairy industries' roles in exacerbating climate change. It gave me one more reason to feel good about veganism—not only was it more compassionate to animals, it was better for the environment.

I eventually met one of the directors of *Cowspiracy*, a guy named Kip Andersen. I gushed to him about how great the film was, and he told me that it was the first in a trilogy of documentaries he was making about veganism. The second, *What the Health*, was going to be about veganism's health benefits. He had me tell the story about walking out of the diabetes fundraiser on camera for that second documentary. But when Lux and I went to go see the finished movie, I felt fucking violated. *What the Health* was basically a vegan propaganda film. It made fairly outrageous claims—among others, that animal protein, not sugar, is really the cause of diabetes, that eating an egg every day is the equivalent of smoking five cigarettes, that milk causes cancer, and that eating fish is toxic. The fact that I was *in* this film made me feel like I was complicit in this nonsense.

Look, there is no doubt that what we eat plays a huge role in the epidemic levels of obesity, diabetes, cancer, and heart disease we see in this country. But rather than stick to the science, this documentary ginned it up, essentially declaring all animal products terrible for your health. It was just a bunch of bullshit, trying to coerce people into becoming vegans on false pretenses.

The film also confirmed a lot of people's negative views of vegans as harsh, uncompromising, and judgmental. It's an unfair generalization, but there are undoubtedly plenty of vegans who fit that mold. I know what it feels like to be on both sides of that. Because I'm such a loud, obnoxious asshole, I touted my veganism to every media outlet that would stick a microphone in my face. That helped make me one of veganism's most visible boosters for quite some time. It also meant that I was constantly having my actions picked over and judged by other vegans on social media. I had people giving me shit over not forcing my cats to be vegan, for fuck's sake. It was all a bit much.

*   *   *

In early 2013, I was flying alone to the tip of Vancouver Island to go surfing by myself. On the Air Canada flight up there, I ordered a Bloody Mary mix—no alcohol, just the mix. The flight attendant told me, "We don't have Bloody Mary mix, only Clamato." My initial reaction was indignation. "But I'm a vegan! I can't drink Clamato! It's made with clams!" She shrugged and continued down the aisle.

The thing is, though, I actually love Clamato. I know a lot of people think it's gross, but in my pre-vegan days, I was very into it. So I started to think about it: One of the go-to guidelines for vegans is always "Don't eat anything with a face." Clams don't have faces. So I asked the flight attendant to go ahead and bring me the Clamato. Some vegans might secretly dream of a nice juicy porterhouse or a roasted turkey leg, but not me: I quit veganism for a plastic cup of Clamato. And it was everything I was hoping for!

That whole surf trip, I continued to guzzle Clamato. After that trip, I had a short residency in Las Vegas, co-headlining comedy shows with Tom Green. One night, he and I were out to dinner with a few other people at a steakhouse. I was still in my head, caught up in my morality drama over the clams. I spent the whole first part of that dinner furiously Googling on my phone "Do vegans eat clams?" and diving deep into vegan online forums looking for an answer. There seemed to be two distinct camps: One camp said that nothing that motivates vegans really applies to clams. The horrors of factory farming don't impact clams because clams actually thrive in factory farm situations. Mercury can be a concern with any kind of shellfish, but clams have such a tiny body that there's not really enough of them to capture mercury. On the positive side of the ledger, I read that clams are richer in iron than a steak. The naysaying camp pointed out that clams will burr themselves into the sediment at the bottom of the ocean to avoid predators, so they clearly value their lives, but to me that seemed more a reflex than a considered thought. When I tallied it all up in my head, I felt okay with my decision to go ahead and order clams.

After that dinner, I started researching crustaceans, and it seemed like the scientific consensus is that they don't have enough of a central nervous system to be able to experience pain. Now I felt comfortable adding shrimp, lobster, and crab to my diet. Not long after that, I was at dinner with my dad and began explaining the winding story behind my new dietary habits. He abruptly cut me off.

"Steve, what the fuck are you doing?" he said.

Dad isn't a vegan and didn't much care what I was eating, but he could see clearly what I was willfully blind to. My fever-ish internet research was really just a manic search for elabo-rate, well-footnoted justifications to do exactly what I wanted to do, which in this case was to eat fish. It had nothing to do with morality. Since then, I've toggled between veganism, vegetarian-ism, and pescetarianism. *Cowspiracy* recharged my veganism for a while, but eventually I got frustrated with the constant criticism and nitpicking from the vegan community. In 2019, I posted an angry rant on social media calling out annoying vegans for polic-ing people like me who essentially agree with them. That post itself engendered even more criticism, which only made me more resentful. It would not be inaccurate to say that spite has fueled a lot of my decisions around veganism since then. When I eat fish or seafood these days, one could argue that I eat it *at* vegans.

*   *   *

The uncomfortable truth about my eating habits is that my ethics are almost always overpowered by deeper, more primal desires. Philosophically, I'm totally against dairy, but I fucking love candy, much of which has milk in it, so I just let that shit slide. Sugar and flour have really been my major issues for a long time. I believe sugar is straight poison for me, but I've had a lot of trouble quit-ting it for good. If you saw how much sweetener I regularly put in my coffee, you would be worried about me. I crave something sweet after a meal the same way I used to crave a cigarette. As soon as I finish a meal, I turn into a fucking werewolf looking for some sort of dessert. And if that dessert has dairy or sugar or flour in it, I don't give a fuck. I will grab a fork and dive right in.

Honestly, I'm a lot luckier than many people in this department. Most of the time, to look at me, you wouldn't know whether I was in a stretch of being a healthy, disciplined eater or if I had been spinning out for months, living on glazed donuts, pizza, and hot sauce. I mean, *I* can notice, but for the most part, I stay reasonably slim. Maybe "slim" is a little too kind. But I don't really get obese. Or I haven't yet. It's the way I *feel* that is the problem. Eating poorly makes me feel awful. *I just chowed down on four Reese's Peanut Butter Cups and half a carrot cake. That is fucked up. I am out of control.* The fact that nobody else in the world may know about it doesn't make me feel any better.

My relationship with food—like so many other people's—is suffused with shame. For example, I want to avoid desserts. When I can't keep myself from eating them anyway, I feel horrible, like a failure. A friend of mine who is a sober alcoholic suggested that it might actually be the shame that I'm jonesing for as much as the sugar. Maybe, his theory goes, I take a perverse pleasure in beating myself up about eating a packet of Reese's Peanut Butter Cups because, on some level, it confirms my own worst opinion of myself. There may be something to that.

The worst part about all the shame is that it saps the pleasure from eating a chocolate cake or a Snickers or a plate of greasy french fries swimming in ketchup. And that fucking blows. If there's anything useful to be taken from all this, it's that the stress we put ourselves under over our shitty eating habits may be just as damaging to us as our shitty eating habits. Stress is a fucking killer. If you add that to the garbage food you're putting into your mouth, it's like you're double-dipping: You're getting fucked up by the food and by the stress. The obvious—though incredibly difficult to implement—solution is that if you're going to eat a carton of ice cream, just eat it and enjoy it. Don't hate yourself for it. You're only human. Plus, there may be no sadder picture in the human experience than of a middle-aged man crying into his tub of Rocky Road. Don't be that guy.

I've done a lot of things to try to control my food problems. For long stretches, I've had a food diary, where I keep track of everything that goes in my mouth, along with its calorie and nutritional information. Of course, that means I'm thinking about food all the fucking time, which itself can be a bit of a problem. I've gone to 12-step meetings for compulsive overeating and spent weeks on end sending photos of every meal to a mentor in one of those groups, but controlling a food addiction is different than controlling a drug addiction. With drugs, the goal is simple: no drugs. With food, the goal is obviously not no food. In this way, it's similar to a sexual addiction in that it's all about finding a healthy way to approach it.

For a guy like me, who is prone to extremes, I find that I need hard-and-fast rules. I need things to be outlawed. Moderation doesn't work. If I'm allowed to eat a slice of bread, I am going to eat half a fucking chocolate cake. So "no flour" is easier for me to cope with than "go easy on the flour."

I also get a strange kick out of following these strictures. It's kind of like my daily schedules or my meditation. I love giving myself the credit for the difficult things I've done. So if I go another day without desserts, that makes me feel like I'm kicking ass.

*   *   *

For all the ink I've already spilled about health in this chapter, the one aspect of it that I haven't directly touched on so far is probably the most important: mental health. In some ways, this entire book is about mental health, but I want to drill down on some specifics here, because this is something I've struggled with quite a bit in my life.

I often say that I'm crazy or that I'm a lunatic, and when I do, yes, I am throwing those words around casually, but also—*I am a fucking lunatic.* The fact that I have been so open in describing the contours of my lunacy doesn't change those contours.

Back when I first got sober, I was diagnosed as bipolar. I chalked that diagnosis up to the fact that anyone who had loaded as many drugs into their body as I had was likely to seem a little bipolar. While I still maintain that to be true, it is also true that I've had both bouts of depression and occasional flights of mania long after all those drugs cleared my system. That depression has occasionally coalesced into thoughts of suicide. Way back in the pre-*Jackass* days, I remember getting as far as thinking about ways I could off myself, and settling, for a moment, on carbon-monoxiding myself to death with my car. Fortunately, at the time, I was so broke, I couldn't even fill the gas tank to start the fucking car, so that idea never came to fruition.

In sobriety, I've faced plenty of dark days too. For a while, my head was pretty fixated on suicide. I don't think I was ever really that serious about it, but I thought a lot about how I could do it in a way so that my body would never be found. I thought about stretches of remote highway where I could go out in the middle of the woods and do the deed. I was imagining a scenario where my death became this big Jimmy Hoffa–esque mystery. The fact that even in this hypothetical I was so concerned with what people might be talking about and thinking about me probably tells you all you need to know about my real motives: I'm an attention whore, even in death.

Around this time, I stumbled on a website about suicide. It had statistics about the success rates of various methods. What I found out is that very few methods are all that reliable. Ones that don't involve a 12-gauge shotgun in your mouth are particularly dodgy. Maybe this is because many of those attempts are a so-called cry for help more than a legit attempt, but whatever the reason, most attempts fail. And when they fail, the results—gruesome injuries, long-term impairment—often seem worse than death. Stumbling on that website kind of scared me straight. Nothing soured me on the idea of killing myself as much as researching ways to kill myself. I just didn't have the stomach for it.

In 2013, a therapist suggested that I get on antidepressants. Initially, I felt like antidepressants were a transgression against my sobriety. But this therapist also identified as a sober alcoholic and told me that Zoloft wasn't something that calls sobriety into question. He was pretty certain it was going to help me.

And it did. I can honestly say that I've never noticed that it made me feel any different whatsoever, but I stopped spending so much goddamn time thinking about suicide. Before I started taking it, comically minor issues would send me into that dark place, but after, those trips were few and far between. I am confident it was the Zoloft that made the difference, because, for a time, I quit taking it, and wouldn't you know it, back came my warped fantasies about sucking on my car's tailpipe. On a practical level, for a guy who takes so much pride in getting shit done, all that suicidal ideation just feels like an unbelievable waste of time. It drives me nuts thinking about all the things I didn't do while thinking about something I was never going to do.

When I think about all this mental health stuff, I'm reminded of something someone told me once: In life, pain is mandatory, but suffering is optional. I think what he meant was that certain things are going to happen whether you like it or not. You'll get old, your muscles won't be as strong as they once were, you might break your leg or get a tumor, you could get fired from your job, someone you love will die. That shit is going to hurt, and it may even hurt for a long time. But whether you allow yourself to suffer, whether you allow the anxiety and stress to compound that pain, that—at least on some level—is a choice.

Hey, I'm no role model for avoiding suffering. I've spent years of my life consumed with anxiety over all sorts of shit, creating a wellspring of suffering for myself and others. Getting a handle on that is, in many ways, my life's work. In fact, it's all our lives' work. Finding a way to be okay with all the bad shit in the world, to make sense of whatever hurt we experience, that's a universal struggle. Learning to deal with pain without turning it into suffering is about the best thing anyone can do for their health. Well, that and flossing.

8

Stand Up for What You Believe In. Just Don't Expect Anyone to Thank You for It.

In late 2011, I got offered a job. It was notable, because this was a job that wasn't going to require me to swim with sharks, set myself on fire, leap into a pile of elephant shit, or put my body at risk in any way. Nope, this was a job where I'd get to encourage *other people* to do fantastically stupid shit and put their bodies at risk.

A production company wanted me to host a game show called *Killer Karaoke* on truTV. There had been a British version of this show already, and the American one was basically teed up and ready to go when they called me. The premise was simple: Contestants attempt to sing their favorite song while enduring a battery of bizarre and sometimes painful challenges. So one guy warbles "On the Road Again" while getting a body wax. Another sings "867-5309/Jenny" as he's wearing several shock collars. A woman tries to make it through "Copacabana" while collecting cash from boxes filled with scorpions, parakeets, and tarantulas. You get the idea. Not exactly high art.

At the time, my career as a stand-up comic was barely a career. I was just starting to tour, and no one was sure if this new undertaking would have legs. Beyond that, my career prospects were looking pretty dim, and I was filled with a shit-ton of anxiety about it. *Jackass 3D* was already well in the rearview mirror, and at that moment it didn't seem all that likely that we'd be doing another movie, at least not for a long time. I hadn't gotten my YouTube channel going yet, and I wasn't really focusing much attention on social media either. I was just kind of sitting around waiting for the phone to ring. So when it rang with this job offer, I was interested. It seemed like hosting a game show wasn't too far removed from stand-up and would be a nice thing to add to the very limited number of jobs I was capable of doing in Hollywood. The show itself also seemed pretty on-brand for me.

I'm telling you all this to try to give you some context for how I got involved with this terrible TV show. And it was terrible. I mean, look, I worked really hard at being a good host, and I think I did okay. Let's just say I don't think I was the primary reason why *Killer Karaoke* sucked.

To be fair, some people liked it. In fact, when it premiered, the *New York Times* gave it a rave review, calling it "the greatest show in television history," with tongue only slightly in cheek. "Since television was invented," the critic Neil Genzlinger wrote, "scripted dramas and comedies have pitted striving humans against an arbitrary universe for entire seasons without saying as much as is conveyed in 10 minutes of this show." Shit, maybe it was high art. But a paragraph later, this astute critic spotted the show's fatal flaw: "It will stop being funny the minute it runs out of tortures to inflict on its contestants and begins repeating itself."

And that's exactly what happened. The creative team had conjured up a very limited number of challenges, so after an episode or two, the whole thing got extremely repetitive. That was the big issue with *Killer Karaoke*. Well, that and the fact that it was a horrific spectacle that celebrated abject cruelty to both humans and animals.

Contestants may have been willing participants, but the ordeals they were put through were kind of traumatic. (One contestant actually sued the show—and me—for an injury she sustained when she slipped and fell on the stage.) Worse than all that, though, was that so many of the challenges involved animals: walking on stink beetles, having pigeons poke at a singer's eyes, being dunked in an icy tank filled with snakes and alligators. I had worked with plenty of animals on *Jackass* and *Wildboyz*, but never doing anything that felt cruel or abusive to them like some of these stunts did. I was a very public animal rights crusader, and although I didn't have any input on these creative decisions, I definitely wasn't stoked about them. But in that moment, I was thinking about how much I wanted to be a team player and impress people with my game show hosting skills. I was thinking about the sorry state of my career. So I said nothing. I just let it slide.

When *Killer Karaoke* aired, the animal rights crowd attacked me, pointing out, for example, that putting cold-blooded snakes in icy water is particularly cruel. I was labeled the World's Worst Animal Rights Advocate. There was a petition that went around calling for me to "stop exploiting animals for profit." You know what? They were right. Sometimes you need people to hold up a mirror for you so you can see what you actually look like, even if it's going to make you feel like shit. And, oh boy, did I ever feel like shit.

Despite all that, the show did well enough to get renewed for a second season. When the planning began for that one, I decided I wouldn't make the same mistake again. I made a point of objecting to all the animal-related challenges. I told the production team that I wouldn't be a part of the show if we continued that stuff. The show's producers considered my principled stand and agreed with me: I wouldn't be a part of the show if they continued that stuff. I got fired, they hired Sugar Ray lead singer Mark McGrath to replace me, and they totally continued that stuff.

I suppose their reaction was foreseeable. Here was this show that had been struggling to come up with creative challenges for its contestants, and suddenly its host was adding to those struggles by declaring more than half of those challenges totally unacceptable. The obvious move in that case is to shit-can the host. I mean, perhaps if I had packaged my problems with the show with a slate of potential solutions—"Here are thirty new ideas for non-animal-related ordeals we can put the contestants through!"—that might have helped. Though, honestly, that wasn't my role, and I'm pretty sure they wouldn't have wanted to hear that shit from me anyway.

It sucked to lose a job at a time when I really needed one, but I was a lot happier with my decision to stand up for what I believed in than I was with my previous decision to look the other way.

No one gave me a medal, animal rights groups didn't suddenly anoint me their Man of the Year, but I had a much easier time looking myself in the mirror. And it didn't even ruin the prospects for my hosting career. The same producer who hired me for *Killer Karaoke* later hired me to host another game show. I may never become the next Ryan Seacrest, but it won't be because of my animal rights protest.

We often fear standing up for what we believe in, and much like I did during season one of *Killer Karaoke*, we often fail at it. It's not just about the noble causes. Sometimes it's about asking for a raise. Or speaking up when you think a project is going off the rails. Or telling your friend that the girl he thinks he's dating is sleeping with somebody else. You have to be willing to live with the fact that no one is going to thank you for being honest and sticking to your guns. In fact, people just might hate you for it.

*   *   *

I've always loved animals, but I can trace my animal rights activism back to my days at Ringling Bros. and Barnum & Bailey Clown College. I wrote all about my clown college days in my first book, and overall it was a pretty great experience. But one day toward the end of my time there, they took a break from all the tumbling and juggling classes and brought in a PR person to school all us clowns on what to say if anyone asked us about animals in the circus. We were told in no uncertain terms that we were to say absolutely nothing. Not a fucking thing. We were clowns. We were supposed to make people laugh. We weren't paid to have opinions.

This PR person went on and on about how the way Ringling

treated elephants—using a bullhook to batter, prod, and drag them around—was perfectly fine. After all, she told us, if any of the elephants were injured or abused, the millions of people who went to the circus every year would all be witnesses. That explanation seemed beyond fishy to me. In fact, that whole day made it feel like Ringling knew they were doing something wrong and were desperately afraid of word getting out.

I filed that away, and about ten years later, I did an interview with PETA about my experiences at clown college and later working at a non-Ringling circus. I was behind the scenes and saw firsthand the inhumane way some circuses treat animals, so I figured I should talk about it. The interview is still online, but it's genuinely painful for me to watch. I was so fucked up at the time—this was nitrous-and-ketamine-era Steve-O—and it's clear that my main motivation was to focus more attention on myself. The cause may have been righteous, but I most certainly was not.

Even if I hadn't been such a douchebag in that interview, it was a pretty low-stakes stand for me to take. I wasn't risking anything by speaking out against Ringling. They didn't employ me, I didn't need anything from them. I mean, there's nothing wrong with speaking out when you have nothing to lose. It's great to take a public stand on an issue you care deeply about. But it doesn't exactly show your mettle, and the danger of becoming a sanctimonious prick—especially for a guy like me—is very real.

All that said, I was pretty stoked when Ringling finally decided to retire elephants from the circus in 2016. The sustained activism—not so much mine as other people's—made a genuine difference. I had mixed feelings about the fact that Ringling shuttered the circus entirely less than a year later. On one level, fuck those bastards, they got what they deserved. But the idea that customers weren't interested in a circus that didn't include elephant abuse bums me out.

*   *   *

I've remained a staunch animal rights activist but tried to put my own spin on my activism. In 2014, inspired in part by the documentary *Blackfish*, which exposed SeaWorld's persistent abuse and mistreatment of orcas, I devised a stunt to focus more attention on the theme park's misdeeds. The plan was to scale a highway exit sign in San Diego near SeaWorld and alter it, so instead of reading "SeaWorld Drive," it would read "SeaWorld Sucks." Okay, it's not the cleverest prank of all time, but it's to the point.

I printed out "SUCKS" on a heavy-duty banner with a green background that would match the highway sign and stocked up on duct tape. I just needed to figure out how to scale the sign to affix this banner to it. I brought a rope, thinking that I'd be able to swing it up onto the sign's ledge and then shimmy up, *Mission Impossible* style. That, it turned out, was way harder than I thought it would be. I spent a few hours struggling to climb this rope to no avail. At one point, I even duct-taped my foot to the rope to try to pull myself up using a sort of pulley system. The net result was me hanging upside down from this rope on the side of the highway. I was frustrated and it was getting dark, so we called it a day.

I came back the next day reinvigorated for the task at hand and bearing a rope ladder that I figured would make the task infinitely easier. And it might have, if the rope ladder didn't snap when I was halfway up it. I landed on my head, which hurt quite a bit, but I was still determined. We made another trip to Home Depot, and this time returned with a long extension ladder, which made scaling the sign remarkably simple and made me wonder why we didn't think of that from the start. I quickly taped up my banner, and for a few hours, anyone driving down I-5 in Mission Bay, California, could clearly see my opinion of SeaWorld. (It sucks.) I recorded the whole episode on video, but it would be months before I posted the video publicly. Believe it or not, I used that time to consult with legal experts about the possibility of SeaWorld suing my ass for the stunt. When I did finally release the video, there was a fair amount of publicity surrounding it. The highway patrol wasn't at all amused and recommended that the DA's office charge me with vandalism and trespassing, though, in the end, all I got was the equivalent of a traffic ticket—two hundred bucks, to be exact. So, yeah, I had raised the stakes on my activism a little, but not much.

The following year, I wanted to do something even bigger. I decided to scale a fifteen-story construction crane in West Hollywood wearing a backpack filled with fireworks and an inflatable orca with "SeaWorld Sucks" written on it. If my highway-sign gag had gotten some attention, *this* would blow people away! The prospect of climbing up that crane was genuinely frightening, so I did some research into cranes the night before and learned about a safety wire that runs along the crane's arm. To this day, I don't believe I've ever publicly admitted that when I was up on top of that crane, I was actually clipped to a wire with a rock-climbing harness that I was wearing underneath my jeans. As soon as I began my incredibly safe walk along the top of that crane, though,

I could see a bevy of firetrucks, police cars, and emergency vehicles gathered down below. In all, eighty firefighters, eighteen cops, a helicopter, and a SWAT team converged on this construction site. I figured that was a good time to start lighting my fireworks! I don't think many of those cops agreed with me. I eventually climbed back down the crane and was promptly arrested.

Right away, I felt bad for wasting all those city resources. Surely those firefighters and cops had better things to do than watch me act like an asshole on top of a one-hundred-and-fifty-foot crane. In a way, the stunt had done what I'd set out to do: It drew a ton of attention and news coverage. But on further reflection, the whole thing was ill-conceived.

Sure, I'd raised the stakes significantly, but why? My entire motivation was suspect. If I'm being totally honest, it had less to do with SeaWorld and much more to do with finding a reason to use this sweet new drone I had just bought. Scott Randolph had learned to fly it, but to get good footage with the drone, I needed to be way up in the air. We looked around, and, lo and behold, there was this construction crane. Climbing it would give us the chance to try out our new toy. But scaling a crane wasn't much of a stunt in and of itself, so I added the inflatable whale with the anti-SeaWorld message, which made it seem like I had a legitimate reason to be up there. I also added the fireworks, which, despite being legitimately nuts, really made no sense whatsoever.

In retrospect, I find that whole crane stunt embarrassing. I mean, I genuinely believe in protesting SeaWorld's treatment of killer whales. I also genuinely believe that climbing that crane and diverting emergency workers from actual emergency work wasn't the way to do it. Both my dad and Johnny Knoxville agreed. In fact, they each called me just after I was released from jail, the day after the stunt, and expressed concern that I'd be made to pay for the resources I wasted. Their estimates were that it could run deep into six figures. I retained the services of an expensive attorney and had him petition the court for jail time for my stunt. He told me I was his first client to ever *request* to be locked up in a cell, but as I explained to him, this was all supposed to be a statement about the cruelty of keeping wild creatures in captivity, so this was my last-ditch effort to make the stunt feel at least kind of clever.

Much to my delight, I was eventually sentenced to thirty days in L.A. County jail, which got even more mainstream global news coverage than I anticipated. I knew damn well that I wouldn't be in there even that long, because the jail was grossly overcrowded and I was not a violent offender. I also knew I'd never be in any danger while I was locked up because I was just famous enough to be sure I'd be in protective custody, which meant little to no contact with other inmates. Still, I figured I'd be in there for at least three or four days before I was released. But after my buddies filmed me doing a backflip off the sign outside the jail and turning myself in, less than eight hours later, they filmed me walking out a free man.

When you strip away all the bullshit, the real driving force behind that stunt was the thing that drives most of my actions: attention. I wanted a viral video. I wanted to be on TMZ. And that brings me to an uncomfortable truth: As much as I genuinely want to shine a light on causes I believe in, most of the time, deep down, I really just want to shine a brighter light on myself.

As unflattering as this is to admit, I'm afraid I'm not alone in this. How often do you see a celebrity or a politician or even just a friend in your social media feed boasting about their good deeds? I mean, there's real activism, and then there's the publicizing of that activism, and the latter has a way of tainting the former. I think we owe it to ourselves to interrogate our own actions before we have any right to do the same to someone else's.

This puts me in a tough spot. I want to be charitable. I want to support the causes I believe in. It genuinely feels good to be doing good in the world. But if you've been reading this book to this point, you know that, at my core, I crave attention like it's fucking oxygen. It is fundamental to my being. But ever since that crane debacle, I've tried to at least check my motivations and acknowledge when they're less than pure. Early in 2021, I made a video that was titled "How I Donated Over $600,000 in 2020." Right at the top of that video, I admitted that it felt weird to be bragging about my charitable work. I was essentially calling myself out for being a bit of a douchebag, before going ahead and being a douchebag anyway. It's an inelegant solution to the problem, but I feel like a little self-awareness goes a long way. In almost any situation, if you can at least acknowledge what you're doing wrong, that may not fix it, but then everyone will understand that you think you're as much of an asshole as they do. Which is not nothing.

Ironically, that video of me raising and donating over half a million dollars to charity during the pandemic generated zero news coverage and garnered less viewership than anything I'd posted on YouTube in years. It turns out that there's not much public appetite for seeing me stand up for what I believe in or do good deeds once the possibility of a spectacular fall from a fifteen-story crane is eliminated. But if I'm doing it for the clout or for a big thank-you, I'm clearly doing it for the wrong reasons. Doing what's right needs to be its own reward, because the only other thing you may get for it is a whole lot of grief.

9

Everyone Needs Someone Who Will Call Them an Asshole

In 2008, when I was at my absolute worst, literally losing my mind on drugs and acting like a vile, maniacal asshole, Johnny Knoxville, Jeff Tremaine, and a bunch of the *Jackass* crew showed up at my apartment and forced me into a psychiatric ward. None of them enjoyed it. They knew I was going to throw a fucking temper tantrum. They knew I'd curse them all out and call them all hypocrites, because, let's face it, none of them were exactly role models for sobriety. But they showed up, told me all the shit I didn't want to hear, and then when I refused to listen, they forced me into the psych ward to sober up so I could start listening.

I look back on what those guys did as one of the most significant acts of friendship in my entire life. At the time, though, I hated them for it. But if I hadn't had people like them in my life—people willing to tell me when I was acting like an asshole and to do something about it—I'd almost certainly be dead. We all should be so lucky to have people around us who love us enough that they're not afraid to make us sometimes hate them.

When I was younger, my friends were often just the people I'd drink with, the people I could rely on to give me drugs, the ones who kissed my ass, or those who wouldn't hassle me about what a colossal dickhead I was becoming. Maybe that's the same for lots of young people. I think many of us look back on the friends we had when we were younger and ask, "Why the fuck was I hanging around with those pricks?" The answer is sometimes as simple as proximity or convenience. Those were the people you went to school with, or the ones you lived in a dorm with, or the crew you worked with. You fall in with a group of friends, and you don't think too much about whether those people enhance your life or detract from it. Maybe that's still your situation, and that's fine, as long as you aren't expecting too much from your friends. But growing older with people around who are willing to both have your back and call you on your bullshit, as the situation demands, is pretty fucking vital.

Once I was in rehab, drying out, my old friend Tommy Caudill came to visit. I'd first met Tommy back in 1997. He started the legendary skatewear brand XYZ with Danny Way and was the first legit business owner to believe in my stunt career. Years before *Jackass* came along, XYZ sponsored me and gave me real opportunities to be seen. Tommy had gotten sober a couple of years before I did and came to see me in rehab to show his support.

Two of the most important things they tell you in recovery are to submit to a higher power and to build a network of people who can help you stay sober. As I mentioned before, my life had become dominated by drug-induced hallucinations that made me feel like I was regularly communing with the supernatural world, so the idea of acknowledging a higher power was no problem whatsoever for me. As far as I was concerned, I'd been chilling with God in my West Hollywood apartment for months.

But the support system was tougher. As much as those *Jackass* guys had saved my life, they were all still getting loaded pretty regularly, so relying on them to bolster my sobriety didn't seem like a winning idea. I remember sitting in that rehab and feeling distinctly like a visitor, an alien in this strange recovery community. What the fuck did I have in common with any of these people? They were accountants and lawyers and teachers and housewives and bus drivers—you know, *regular* people. I, most certainly, was not. I was out of my element.

Tommy, though, was fucking rad. His visit helped change my perspective and open my eyes. He told me his story and explained that I had to make protecting my sobriety the biggest priority in my life. "You're gonna find out who your real friends are," he said. "Anybody who is clowning on your sobriety, that motherfucker is not your friend. Those people want you dead." He said this with the utmost seriousness but also made me realize that there were plenty of my kind of people in recovery. What's more, many of those who didn't seem like they were my kind of people probably had a lot more in common with me than I knew. His visit made me feel like I belonged where I was. I wasn't an alien anymore. There was a real path forward.

*   *   *

Maintaining sobriety has taught me a lot about the importance of creating support systems and leaning on other people. The other side of that, which is just as important, is being the kind of person who can offer guidance and support and be an example to others. In other words, if you sometimes need people around to call you an asshole, you also sometimes need to be the person willing to call someone else an asshole. I take that role seriously. Tommy and many others have done that for me, and, in turn, I've tried to do that for others.

In late 2016, Tommy Lee from Mötley Crüe shared a video on social media of a heavyset kid in Indiana who attached a ton of fireworks to his bare body, lit them all, and called it "The Suicide Vest." In the years since *Jackass* came out, and particularly since the rise of YouTube and Instagram, there have been countless kids who have posted videos of themselves doing *Jackass*-like stunts. I have rarely ever publicly encouraged or endorsed *Jackass* copycats—not for moral reasons, but because I just found most of that stuff to be unbearably lame. This was the first time I saw something that blew me away to such an extent that I actually wanted to meet the person behind it. The fact that he was wearing an XYZ hat in the video just made it seem like it was meant to be. So I flew this kid, Zach Holmes, out to L.A.

I loved Zach immediately and quickly came up with an idea for a stunt he could do on a hiking trail near my house. We built a janky wooden ramp so he could jump over this thirty-foot-long patch of cacti on a skateboard. We both knew without question that he would never be able to jump so much as a foot, which is why the idea was so funny in the first place. The inevitable result—him toppling facefirst into a massive cactus patch wearing nothing but goggles and a speedo—was nothing short of disastrous. When we pulled him out, he was a fucking mess, with hundreds of cactus needles stuck into him. I was worried he might get a staph infection, so the following day I took him to an urgent care clinic. As it turned out, the doctors were more concerned about his sunburn than the needles. They gave him some antibiotics and sent him on his way.

Nonetheless, I felt legitimately bad for my role in getting him impaled with all those needles. It occurred to me that I needed to do more to point this kid in the right direction. It didn't take a detective to see that Zach was in bad shape. I'm not talking about the cactus needles and the sunburn: Zach was wildly overweight, and a lot of the stunts he was doing were *dark*. So many of them involved him hurting himself for the amusement of others, which, of course, I could relate to. As I got to know him, I could see that, in a lot of ways, he was frighteningly like me when I was hurtling through my twenties, dead certain I wouldn't live to see thirty. I felt like I was in a unique position to help him.

Before he left L.A., I had a long talk with Zach and told him all my concerns but also my vision for what he could be. He needed to get healthy. The market for people who wanted to see him get seriously hurt was limited and creepy, but if he could transform himself, the world would really open up for him. I told him I wanted to help, and he was immediately jazzed on the idea.

Zach moved out to California and kind of became my project. We started calling him Zackass. I got him into a program to deal with his food issues, and into a sober-living house. He was offered a *Jackass*-like MTV show called *Too Stupid to Die*, and I helped him with the contracts for it. I bought him a used car, but when he drove it off the lot, I got a sense that this project might be more challenging than I'd first envisioned. I was in the passenger seat, and Zach was just blowing through red lights. He was out of it. I'd thought his main issues were food and obesity, but Zach was a full-blown drug addict. Learning that didn't discourage me from trying to help Zach at all. In fact, it made me feel like I was even better suited to do so. I had a good support group in place, guys like Tommy and Scott Randolph, and we went all in, not just to help him get sober and healthy, but to give him guidance in his stunt career.

At a certain point, I had an idea for a stunt that Zach and I could do together for his MTV show. The premise was to do a seemingly reckless stunt in my living room but use the best pyrotechnic guys in Hollywood. I hired this team of pyro pros and had the whole thing arranged and ready to go. The night before we were set to do the stunt, I invited the whole crew over to my place for dinner and a meeting to go over the plan. Zach had been checked out for weeks, and he didn't say a word throughout the dinner, even though the only topic of conversation was filming the next day for his show. I was questioning the whole project I had undertaken with him. I'd spent a lot of money, time, and energy on him, and he couldn't even be bothered to participate in planning a stunt that we were doing for *his* show? I thought about it and decided to just do the stunt myself. Zach wouldn't even be on camera.

It was a hard decision, but I felt like continuing to reward him for bad behavior was doing more harm than good. The best thing I could do for him, as a mentor and as a friend, was to tell him he was fucking up and to create real consequences. In that moment, I felt like he needed me to call him an asshole. He took it in stride and told me he understood. Which is a diplomatic way of saying he was too far gone to really much care.

The whole experience with Zach was also an important reminder that you can't make someone else want to get sober. It just doesn't work that way. We had all the architecture in place, we were saying the right things, but Zach wasn't ready. It's not just sobriety that you can't force on people. As much as you might want to change someone's life, as much as you have a benevolent vision for their future, if they don't want it for themselves, it's a dead end.

When I think back on it now, the offer I made to help Zach was naive. Here was this kid who had been struggling, making home stunt videos in Bumfuck, Indiana, and suddenly I ride in on my white horse and extend a hand. He had grown up watching *Jackass*, wanting to emulate us, and now one of those people he'd been emulating is offering him the world. What the fuck do you think he's going to say? "No thanks, Steve-O. I'd prefer to stay in my little town and get fucked up with my friends." Of course not.

Fortunately, Zach did come around eventually, albeit on his own timetable. He called me a couple years later. He was sober, in a 12-step program, and working his ninth step, making amends. He sincerely and thoroughly took responsibility for being such a fucking pain in the ass when I was trying to help him. He thanked me for being a real friend and calling him out when he needed to be called out. I was really impressed with him, and I'm completely fucking stoked that he became one of the new cast members for the fourth *Jackass* film. It felt like that project I'd undertaken with him had borne fruit, even if it hadn't happened exactly the way I'd planned.

*   *   *

Interestingly, that pyro shoot I had planned to do with Zach involved a series of stunts that culminated in one that I've referred to a few times in this book already: doing snow angels in rocket fuel on my floor. It didn't work out so great for me. For trying to be a good friend and mentor to Zach, I ended up with serious burns, which required skin graft surgery on fifteen percent of my body. No good deed goes unpunished, I guess.

In the aftermath of that stunt, when my burns were getting more and more agonizing, I needed something to take my mind off the pain, so I decided to go on Instagram Live. Scott Randolph was holding my iPhone, filming me, and initially I was just answering questions from fans and talking about how I'd gotten burned. But the pain was excruciating, and I feel like it induced some sort of manic episode. It triggered memories of the pain my mom endured after she'd had a brain aneurysm years before. Soon enough, I was hysterically bawling on this livestream, talking about my mom and how I'd never fully dealt with her death. Despite my pain—or maybe because of it—I felt spiritually plugged in as all this was happening, but not really in a good way. Judging by the comments, to most people it seemed like I was losing my mind. It was reminiscent of the experiences I'd had on nitrous and ketamine, but without any drugs.

All this put Scott in a very awkward position. As he was film-ing this on my phone, he was getting a steady stream of texts on his phone from my friends asking him if I was okay, telling him he needed to stop streaming this breakdown and get me some help. Which is exactly what I'm sure he would've done except for the fact that I was simultaneously telling him *not* to stop filming. For whatever reason—or maybe for the same attention-seeking reason I do everything—I wanted this emotional crack-up to be public. Further complicating Scott's position was that in addition to being one of my closest friends in the world, Scott also works for me. So, in that moment, is he supposed to be Scott my empa-thetic friend who wants to help or Scott my kickass employee who knows the first rule of working for me is to never stop filming?

This, I suppose, is one of the perils of working with friends, though when I first hired him, Scott was a stranger. In the early days of my sexual sobriety, I had been looking for a sober com-panion, someone to be around when I was touring who would keep me from getting my dick sucked. Scott was not the first person I hired to do this prestigious work. The first guy I hired was an aspiring actor. I drove up to San Francisco with him to do some shows, and it was a nightmare. I was paying this guy five hundred bucks a day, and he was just obnoxious, jamming his cell phone in my face while I was driving so I could see videos of him acting. I tried another guy who wasn't nearly as bad, but we didn't really click, and then finally I called Scott, who joined me for some dates in Tennessee. At the time, Scott was working as a bartender, but it was obvious that he was smart, entrepreneurial, and an all-around good person. We hit it off right away, and in short order, he not only became one of my best friends, he became a vital and transformative part of my business operation. Which is what brought him to the ethical crossroads he eventually arrived at, pointing that iPhone at me while I fell apart.

Scott's in recovery too, so rigorous honesty is as important to him as it is to me. He is definitely not a yes-man. When I have a bad idea, he'll be the first to tell me. In some ways, I think our tight bond makes him feel more comfortable telling me hard truths. He knows me well enough to know I'm not going to fire him for telling me something I don't want to hear.

In the case of this livestream, it did go on for about forty-five minutes, but eventually Scott got me off it by telling me that Lux was calling and needed to talk to me. The truth is, he had texted Lux to tell her to call with the express purpose of gently easing me off the livestream. If he hadn't been a friend who knew me, I'm not sure he could've finessed that.

The funny thing about Scott and me is that although we have plenty in common, we're very different too. We both like to work twenty-four hours a day, but Scott is detailed and precise. Some might say anal. He makes sure all the T's are crossed and the I's are dotted. Before he undertakes a project, he makes sure he's done all his research and is totally prepared for any eventuality. Me, on the other hand, I'm all over the fucking place. I'm more of a "Ready, fire, aim" kind of guy. I get ideas and just want to do them right away. When I had Mark Cuban on my podcast, he told me he was the same way and hired people who balanced him out.

It seems like such a basic idea, but I think you've got to know your strengths and weaknesses, then find people to work with—and to just *be* with—who can cover what you're not good at. You don't really need someone around to do what you can already do or to tell you how great you're doing it. If I have one genuine piece of business advice to offer in this book, that's it: Work with people who complement you, not ones who compliment you.

*   *   *

Working with friends can be complicated, but I'm not sure I'd want it any other way. I consider the *Jackass* crew to be among my closest friends in the world, but those are also work relationships, which can make them a fucking bitch to navigate. That cliché about how money can ruin friendships has a lot of truth in it.

The thing about *Jackass* is that while it has been extraordinarily successful, it is not as if we have all shared equally in that success. As *Jackass*'s creators and producers, Johnny Knoxville, Jeff Tremaine, and their third partner, Spike Jonze, have gotten obnoxiously rich, while some of the cast members have struggled to make a decent living.

I don't say this as a knock against Knoxville and Tremaine: They've done much more work and they deserve more money. But let's just say that in the decade after *Jackass 3D* came out, there were a lot of emails going around among the core *Jackass* members about whether to do another film. Some of the guys would make the point that fans were constantly asking for another film.

For a long time, Knoxville's response was always some version of "I'd rather leave people asking for another film than to have them asking why we made the last film." It was a totally fair point—leave 'em wanting more—but also one that ignored the financial reality that some of the cast members were facing. They had bills to pay and families to support. They *needed* another film, and they felt like this guy who was supposed to be their friend wasn't helping them out.

When the fourth film, *Jackass Forever*, finally became a reality, there were a lot of sighs of relief among the cast. I was in a slightly different position. I had spent the previous decade building my business. I had done other TV shows. I had branched out into stand-up, created a profitable YouTube channel, and had millions more social media followers than anyone else in the *Jackass* cast, including Knoxville. I was selling tens of thousands of dollars in merch every month. All my workaholic insanity had begun to pay off, and while I was stoked to do another *Jackass* film, I was not in the same financial straits as a few of the other cast members.

I was also in a much different situation than I had been in when *Jackass 3D* came around a decade earlier. Back then, I was newly sober and had no real sense of what my future might hold. I felt like a shell of myself. My mental state was rickety, and I thought it was entirely possible that my career was done. So, against the loud and sustained advice of my lawyer, I essentially agreed to the first contract that was sent to me. In fact, I rushed to sign it. I later came to regret not negotiating at all, and, rightly or wrongly, felt like I'd been railroaded a little.

Because I'm a bitch that holds a grudge, all that was still on my mind when it came time to work out our *Jackass Forever* contracts. This time I was determined that I was not going to get rolled so easily. I may have overcompensated.

Initially, I felt like the producers were trying to lowball me. They were crying poverty, but I felt like I understood the truth: They had made their deal with Paramount, and whatever they paid us was coming out of their end. They were being greedy. Their offer to me felt like they were disrespecting the work I'd been putting in during the ten years since we'd made *Jackass 3D*. I made the case that with the platform I had built over the past decade, I brought more to the table than I had in the past. So I said no to the contract they offered. Again and again, I said no.

This didn't make anyone happy with me. The rest of the *Jackass* guys were exasperated. I was made to feel like an ungrateful, selfish dick who didn't care about his friends. And maybe I was acting like an ungrateful, selfish dick. I was certainly being reckless with the relationships that had, to that point, been among the most important in my life. I know Knoxville was getting pissed off with me. But I held firm. I felt like they needed me more than I needed them, and I told them as much. I kept pushing. Production started without me.

Things got very tense between us. During their first week of test shoots, which I wasn't there for since I had not signed a contract (but which I heard all about through friends on set), Knoxville got in front of the camera to introduce the first stunt they'd filmed in years. He mentioned that he had so many ideas for stunts over the previous ten years that he had wanted to film, and then proceeded to introduce one that he called "Fire in the Hole." In the stunt, multiple cast members inserted a funnel into their asses and then poured in hot sauce. Great stunt, right? Except I had posted the *exact same stunt* nearly a year earlier on You-Tube to promote my own hot sauce, which is actually called... wait for it...HOT SAUCE FOR YOUR BUTTHOLE! I drove traffic toward that video with all my social media. Knoxville had even liked and commented on the stunt when I posted it. So what the fuck was this? Were they were just trying to stick it to me? Was this a hardball negotiation tactic? I was flabbergasted and fuming.

This contract stalemate dragged out for a while. I told them that I was okay if the movie happened and I wasn't in it. I did a few interviews in which I said basically the same thing. I tried hard to convince myself that this was, in fact, true. Really, deep down, it probably would have crushed me to know that they were doing *Jackass* and I wasn't part of it.

Fortunately, that didn't happen. Cooler heads prevailed. Compromises were made. While it was true that I had a bigger platform to bring to the film, it was also true that my bigger platform was going to put me in a position to reap bigger rewards from the movie's success. In the end, I don't think it was ever really about wanting more money, so much as it was about wanting acknowledgment and recognition from Knoxville and Tremaine that I had done well for myself in the previous ten years, that I had really built something. That and to somehow make up for the fact that I hadn't fought for my own interests on *Jackass 3D*.

I don't think any of this haggling is particularly unusual for a Hollywood film. But it's necessary context for what happened next. When I showed up on the set of *Jackass*, there was a little tension, but within a day or two, it had dissipated and we were back to our normal selves, doing stupid shit with and to each other. It felt good to know that the friendship endured. I distinctly remember one of the first stunts I did, strapping a tiny box with a queen bee onto my dick, which then attracted thousands more bees, which eventually started stinging me. As I stood there with what looked like an elephant trunk made of bees hanging from my dick and all my buddies standing around laughing about it, I felt like all was right with the world again.

Then I fucked it up. I had filmed for about a week when COVID shut down the shoot for a few months and everyone went into lockdown. Shortly before we went back into production, I went on a podcast and recounted this whole negotiation, even though the negotiation was over and it made no sense to talk about it publicly. I was digging at old wounds that weren't fully healed. I worry that I'm doing it again now in this book, but my motivation this time is completely different. In trying to make my case on that podcast for why I deserved more money, I said, "Over the last ten years, I've stayed active, and—without being a dick—I'm the only guy that's been active. I think it's safe to say that at this point, I bring more to the table than the rest of the guys."

The fact that I used the phrase "without being a dick" was a surefire tell that I knew I was being a dick. My defense was that what I said was, on its face, largely true, and not in a way that necessarily speaks well of my emotional health. I had spent the last ten years chasing something, trying to prove something to somebody, trying to stay relevant, while most of the rest of the cast were content and happy with who they were. In many ways, I envy their peace of mind. All that said, to come out and air that dirty laundry was just fucking stupid and unnecessary. I was still grasping for recognition, for affirmation, in a way that was venal, careless, and destructive. That sound bite quickly made its way back to the *Jackass* cast and was shared in our group text. People were fucking unhappy with me, and I understood why.

When production restarted, I slunk back onto set and did the only thing I could do: apologize. I went around to each of the guys and admitted that, as much as I want to be able to defend myself, the fact is, I'm a douche, I've always been a douche, and I'm sorry. To their credit, none of them held a grudge, and everyone quickly put it behind them.

Well, almost everyone. If I'm being honest, my whole contract holdout, the reasons behind it, and the callous disregard I showed for the most important friendships in my life, it all still ate at me for weeks while we were filming. One day, I called Knoxville and spilled my regrets about how I'd handled the negotiations. For as much progress as I'd made toward being healthy and well adjusted, I told him, I was still very much a pitiful, needy creep at my core. *Jackass* has always been very much like being in a band. We're a bunch of guys who have known each other for most of our adult lives. We love each other, but we're also in business together. I recognized that, in the proverbial *Behind the Music* episode about this band, I was the asshole who was bringing all the negative energy that was going to break up the group.

It was only the fact that the rest of the guys were healthy enough that this band was able to survive it. I told Knoxville how profoundly grateful I was for that.

Knoxville got choked up. He told me I was being too hard on myself, but that it was a rare person who was willing to take a hard look in the mirror and make this sort of phone call. Most people just stuff it down and move on. He took responsibility for his part too, admitting he was not the easiest guy to deal with either. It was a powerful conversation that really cleared the air between us and made me feel like our relationship was stronger than it had ever been. I had similar conversations with Tremaine and Spike.

It goes back to what I was saying before about being your own harshest critic and being candid about your shortcomings. I don't mean just doing this as a sort of performative act, but there is something extremely powerful about *not* defending or justifying your actions, about trying to see yourself as the asshole that other people may be seeing. It's fucking liberating. I've needed Knoxville, Tremaine, Spike, and all those guys to call me on my bullshit so many times in my life, but I think it was even more meaningful when I was finally grown up enough to call myself on it.

Interestingly, that hot sauce bit that they did without me never made it into *Jackass Forever*. But when I attended a screening of *Jackass 4.5*—a streaming release that tells the behind-the-scenes story of the making of *Jackass Forever*, complete with lots of unseen stunt footage that didn't make the cut for the theatrical release—the very first bit was the hot sauce stunt, complete with Knoxville's intro. There was no mention of my hot sauce or that it was originally my bit.

I lost my shit. For one, this was a blatant theft of my intellectual property. Beyond that, it just felt like a hard "fuck you" at me. And, keep in mind, this was not an early, unedited cut of the film. This was a locked, mixed, finished movie. And I had even talked to Tremaine about the possibility of plugging my hot sauce in the movie. So this made me feel seriously fucking violated.

I raised holy hell about it. The *Jackass* producers quickly backed down and profusely apologized. Spike sent me a long message telling me that it was not done maliciously but was incredibly thoughtless, and that they felt horrible about it. They offered to recut the bit, adding a voiceover that credited me with the idea and showing a clip of my stunt, as well as my hot sauce.

I thought about all this for a minute. It felt fair. It's a big fucking deal to unlock a finished picture and make changes to it. It costs money. I'm still not certain that including that hot sauce bit in the first place wasn't done with some deliberate intent to needle me for my contract holdout, but in the same way that they'd all accepted my apology after I'd bad-mouthed them on a podcast, I realized it was incumbent on me to let it go. I suppose the other side of being willing to call your friends out for being assholes is being willing to accept their apologies when they own up to it.

*   *   *

As it turned out, my contract holdout and blundering negotiation was not the most tumultuous personnel upheaval around *Jackass Forever*. Not even close. All my bullshit may have tested the strength of the bonds between the *Jackass* crew, but what has happened with Bam Margera has shaken those bonds to their core.

This is a really hard thing to write about, not just because in many ways it is still going on, but also because I fucking love Bam. From day one of *Jackass*, I looked at him as being better than me on so many levels: He was smarter, more charismatic, funnier, and insanely entrepreneurial. Without a doubt, at times my admiration could be flecked with jealousy, and for sure, in the early days, Bam often couldn't fucking stand me. But we've always had a lot in common, both good and bad, and eventually built a real and deep friendship. As the title of this chapter suggests, though, what we sometimes need from our real friends is a dose of hard truth. Of course, calling someone an asshole when they need to hear it does not necessarily mean that they will listen.

I'm not going to recount the history of Bam's issues with booze, drugs, and mental health. That's his story to tell. But suffice to say, there are real issues, they have been long-running, and anyone who has even a passing familiarity with TMZ will be aware of them. He's been to many rehabs, he's been in psych wards, and I've tried to be there with him—to the extent that's possible—to help guide him through, in the way that guys like Tommy did for me. But as of the moment I'm writing this sentence, sobriety has not really stuck for Bam yet. Without naming names, he's had a lot of people around him who do not have his best interests in mind and who, in fact, seem to be leeching off him, trying to prop him up *Weekend at Bernie's* style to keep the money tap flowing. Even plenty of people who genuinely care about him haven't been willing to call him out and hold him accountable.

When it came time to make this latest *Jackass* film, the producers were well aware of Bam's substance abuse issues and were sincerely worried about him. As such, they wrote an amendment to his contract that required him to stay sober and to prove he was staying sober by submitting to regular drug tests. He didn't live up to those conditions, and Tremaine, Knoxville, and Spike were faced with a decision as to what to do about it.

It was an agonizing choice with no good options. Bam had already filmed a few bits, including one they talked about calling "The Silence of the Bam": him walking through a pitch-black house while being terrorized by Knoxville, who was wearing night-vision goggles. Tremaine told me it was the funniest thing they'd ever filmed. A bunch of us also did a thing where we hopped on an industrial-strength treadmill while carrying marching band equipment. I mentioned this one early in the book: I got knocked out cold and taken to the hospital. That footage was badass too.

So, on a practical level, firing Bam and cutting him out of the movie meant losing some great material. It also meant that when the film came out, the first question everyone would ask would be "Why isn't Bam in it?" It would be a huge distraction. And it would undoubtedly have an effect on Bam too. Financially, he'd take a huge hit, and being fired would be humiliating for him in a very public way. Some people thought being cut out of *Jackass* could actually kill him. I can only imagine how it would feel if something horrible like that were to happen.

On the other hand, someone needed to set boundaries in Bam's life and enforce them. If there were consistently no consequences for his behavior, if the people around him kept making excuses, we would be enabling his substance abuse. If we really cared about him, his health was more important than this movie, and certainly more important than any uncomfortable interviews we might have to do.

Look, it's unbelievably hard when someone you love is an addict. You are faced with horrible choices daily. Parents have to turn their kids out into the street or refuse to bail them out of jail even though every fiber of their being is telling them to do otherwise. Without support, without guidance, making those kinds of decisions is unbearable.

With Bam, none of this was my decision to make, but because of my experiences in rehab and the psych ward, my opinion was frequently solicited and probably held some sway. I was torn, and for a while I was somewhat surprisingly arguing for Bam to be given another chance. At various points, he was trying to stay sober, and I thought the damage from cutting him loose could be worse than the damage from keeping him involved. I thought maybe there was an in-between solution—firing him, creating some financial consequences, but still allowing the bits he'd filmed to be in the movie. (I also worry that the attention-seeking part of me just didn't want to lose the marching band stunt that sent me to the hospital.) Behind the scenes, I spoke to and texted with Bam daily, trying to keep him committed to sobriety and counseling him on how to approach Tremaine, Knoxville, and Spike about getting back on board with the film. I was practically writing scripts of what to tell them that would convince them he was committed to getting healthy.

Ultimately, though, not unlike the situation with Zach, Bam really wasn't ready to hear that message. He blamed the producers for putting him through a battery of unfair drug tests. He felt like he was being singled out. He told me that he just wanted to put this all behind him and get back to filming. To me, it felt like he was still in denial about how serious this really was. At one point, he had a call scheduled with Tremaine, Knoxville, and Spike to talk about a way forward for him and he showed up visibly wasted on social media before failing to join the call. Essentially, he made their decision for them. He was out.

It's unsurprising that Bam responded to getting fired by lashing out. He tried to rally people to boycott *Jackass Forever*, he trashed Knoxville, Tremaine, and Spike on social media, and he sued them and Paramount for what he claimed was wrongful termination. I think back to when those same guys came to my apartment and forced me into the psych ward to get me sober. I thought they were ganging up on me and unfairly singling me out. I thought I knew better. I was pissed. I was lashing out. It was only because they threatened to physically drag me out of that apartment that I finally relented. Even then, I figured I was just going along with them until I could weasel my way out of the psych ward and back into the loving arms of my drug addiction.

Fortunately for me, my life had unraveled to such a degree that when I dried out even a little, I could recognize the gravity of the situation. My inability to function at all as a rock-bottom alcoholic drug addict made me lucky. For me, it was sobriety or death. Bam has bumbled along with drugs and alcohol for longer than I ever did. At times, he's held it together and been somewhat functional, which has perhaps made getting sober all that much harder for him. In this way, rock bottom can be a gift. It's a long, slow ride down if you never hit that bottom.

I guess what I'm getting at is that I can only hope that Bam will one day look back on the *Jackass* family exiling him from *Jackass Forever* the same way I look back on them forcing me into rehab: as an act of the most extreme love possible. It tracks back to the previous chapter, about standing up for what you believe in without any expectation that you'll be thanked for it. Doing that for the people close to you, at the risk of pushing them away forever, is selfless, thankless, and the true measure of a friend. I am here today because I had people willing to tell me what an asshole I was and how I was killing myself. We all need that in our lives, even if—no, *especially* if—we don't really want it.

10

Your Legacy Is Bullshit

Human existence is all a bit of a cruel prank. I mentioned this earlier in the book: Our most basic human instinct is to survive and the one guarantee life provides is that we won't. Fuuuuuck, that sucks. One way to think about the entire human experience is that it's all an exercise in coming to terms with that paradox. When every fiber of your being cries out for something—not dying—that you know you'll never achieve, how do you find a way to be okay with that? How do we give our lives meaning when, in the grand scheme of things, it all seems so pointless?

I imagine people have been wrestling with these questions ever since there were people. Once cavemen grasped the fact that they were all one day going to die, it couldn't have been long before Ogg, Ugg, and the rest of the gang started painting on the walls of their cave, praying to unseen gods, and naming their kids things like Ogg Jr. In the face of life's big riddle, it's hard not to get obsessed with what we're going to leave behind after we're gone.

That was a big part of the reason I turned the video camera

on myself when I was a teenager. It felt like a way out of the oh-shit-I'm-gonna-die-one-day conundrum. My footage was going to be my message in a bottle to future generations, my proclamation that "Yes, Steve-O was once here on this Earth" and "Yes, he did staple his scrotum to his leg. Multiple times, in fact." Those stunt videos were going to be my cave paintings. Da Vinci painted the *Mona Lisa*; I chugged beer up my own asshole with a funnel. We are both artists in our own way.

With all due respect to scientific advances in cryogenics and artificial intelligence, man hasn't really made any huge strides since the caveman days in how we think about life after death. You can have children so a part of you lives on. You can lean on religion because most religions exist to make you feel better about death by promising heaven or some other afterlife prize. Or you can try to leave something interesting behind. That last one always seemed to fit best for me.

I remember when I was at clown college, one night I was drunk and babbling confidently about how I had all this rad video footage that was going to live on after I was gone and make me immortal. This marine biology student listened to me patiently and then when I was done, shook her head sadly. "You're pathetic," she said. "You're so self-absorbed. How about if I help preserve a coral reef, and every time an organism feeds on that coral reef, *I'm* still alive. Isn't that a more worthwhile legacy? It doesn't have to all be about you, you, you."

Her point was a decent one, though, obviously, she didn't know me very well. At that time in my life, everything *was* all about me, me, me. These days, it's only a little bit less so.

*   *   *

On one level, I completely agree with the title of this chapter: The entire idea of caring about your personal legacy is bullshit. I'm not saying we shouldn't think about future generations—not at all—but any time spent fretting over how future generations will think of *you* is like masturbation for your ego: somewhat gratifying but kind of a waste of time. I mean, what do you care what everyone is saying about you after you're gone? It shouldn't matter to you, douchebag. You're dead.

Except, while I logically know all of that to be true, the self-obsessed attention whore in me can't help thinking rather compulsively about my legacy. I mean, what other possible reason could there be for me to spend endless hours trying to perfect every YouTube video I post? This is a medium that is supposed to be transitory practically by definition, but deep down, the way I think about those videos, or any video footage, hasn't really changed since I explained it to that annoyed marine biology student. I still hope it will make me immortal.

The thing is, those VHS tapes that I filmed my first footage on would be virtually unwatchable now if I hadn't been around to convert them to a new digital format. Even if you could hunt down a VHS player, the tapes degrade over time. Ditto for my early DVDs. I expect that media will continue to evolve and eventually I'll be scrambling to preserve my YouTube archive on another format, not to mention trying to promote it. Then, one day, I won't be around to do even that, and who knows if anyone else will care enough to do it for me.

On an intellectual level, I know that we are all destined to be forgotten; it's just a matter of how quickly. In two hundred and fifty years, how many entertainers from this era will still be recognized or talked about? Well, think about it like this: How many entertainers can you name from the 1770s? Granted, entertainment is a bigger part of our culture than it was two hundred and fifty years ago, but still, how many from today will be being talked about in the 2270s? Five? Ten? That means in the battle for long-term relevance, I'm going to have to somehow elbow out Taylor Swift, Beyoncé, Brad Pitt, Dave Chappelle, Kim Kardashian, and many, many others. I know not many would bet on that happening, but I haven't given up hope. When you think of some of the most famous entertainment figures from the late-nineteenth and early-twentieth century, people like Harry Houdini or P. T. Barnum, they weren't necessarily the most accomplished people. They were the ones who were best at promoting and publicizing their work. They were, in essence, the self-obsessed attention whores of their day. You can probably see where I'm going with this: Maybe there's a chance for me!

All that said, the older I get, the more I think about what that marine biology student told me about saving a coral reef, and the more that concept makes sense to me. That cliché about leaving the world a better place than you found it is a pretty hopeless task for anyone in my generation, seeing as how we've fucked things up so badly over the past forty years. But that doesn't mean you can't leave a small corner of it better than when you found it. I already talked about my SeaWorld protests and have peppered stories of my charitable giving into this book in a way that is probably stomach-turningly self-congratulatory. But I do think that part of the reason why doing good in these ways *feels* so good is because we are doing something that can resonate even after we're gone. We're solving just a little piece of that dreaded existential puzzle.

If I have one long-term project that I hope will be my version of that restored coral reef, it's the animal sanctuary that Lux and I are planning to open. We've been taking baby steps toward it for a while. We've shopped for plots of land and explored ways that we can make it sustainable as a nonprofit. We've tried to learn how to run the sanctuary ourselves and acquired three goats who live in a small barn at our home in the Hollywood Hills as a kind of sanctuary starter kit. Once we've got the land, Lux and I will finally get married on it. That's the plan.

When I think about it like that, the sanctuary does sort of feel like a classic legacy project, both personally and professionally. If we do it right, it will be a place that can outlive me and can rescue animals long after I'm dead. If I do it wrong, it will be a boondoggle that eats up all my savings during the years when I'll need those savings the most. As such, it's a high-risk, high-reward endeavor, but that's been the case with pretty much every worthwhile stunt that I've done in my life so far.

*   *   *

I remember hearing this joke when I was in seventh grade that stuck with me: What is the definition of macho? A man who jogs home from his own vasectomy. It's not the greatest joke, and I'm betting that when I first heard it, I didn't even know what a vasectomy was. But back then, I really wanted to be macho, so I knew that at some point I was going to get a vasectomy, and afterward, I was going to do something way more badass than just jog home. As I got older, my ideas about manhood evolved. Particularly with

Jackass, we've always subtly tweaked what it means to be macho, adding gleeful doses of homoerotic nudity and cross-dressing that probably have made some of our fans uncomfortable. That evolution made me think about that old joke a little differently, and I came up with a far sillier spin: If a real man jogs home from his own vasectomy, I wanted to do an Olympiad after mine.

I told this idea to my father when I first thought of it, way back in 2002. My dad is not a particularly emotional guy, but of all the crazy shit that I've done or even talked to him about doing, I'd never seen him get so upset about a stunt idea as he did about that one. He didn't care about the Olympiad part of it, but he was wildly disturbed that I might never have kids. "You and your sister are the best things that have ever happened to me," he said. "I would hate for you to be denied that same sort of richness in your life." Keep in mind that he told me this back when I was still a drug-addled pain in the ass. To steal Seth Rogen's joke from *Knocked Up*, if I was the *best* thing that ever happened to my dad, I felt bad for Dad. In all seriousness, things could've easily gone another way for me. Twenty years ago, I think the good money would've been on me dropping dead of a drug overdose, dying in some tragically stupid accident, or spiraling into a depressing, debilitating, and infuriating cycle of long-term addiction. It could've been a lifetime of pain and heartbreak for my dad. In many ways, he barely dodged a bullet.

Nonetheless, I took his words to heart and filed that stunt away. I wasn't in any rush to get my balls chopped, and I probably should not have been making that sort of permanent decision back when I was on drugs anyway. Then, a few years ago, I took it back off the shelf and thought long and hard about it.

For most people, the simplest way to create a legacy is to have children. With that, you are literally passing on your DNA, ensuring that your bloodline continues. But as much as it bums my dad out, I never want to have kids. I'm not being self-deprecating when I say I don't think my genes are something that should really be passed on. We can argue until we're blue in the face about nature versus nurture, but you will never convince me that my penchant for addiction and wanton, attention-seeking stupidity doesn't have a strong genetic basis. My mom was an alcoholic who came from a long line of people with similar pre-dispositions. I see other relatives of mine who have the same dis-comfort in their own skin that has plagued me since childhood. Passing all that on to someone else feels downright cruel.

That's really only a part of my calculation, though. Looking at the state of humanity right now, you could argue that having kids is an act of defiant optimism, though I might argue it's closer to stubborn delusion. I mean, once you bring your bundle of joy home from the hospital, what does it have waiting for it but a life-time of steadily worsening environmental catastrophes, political polarization, and economic inequality? *Yeah, thanks for all that, Pops!* I really feel like my conscience couldn't handle bringing a person into a world where the rich continue to get richer and the incredibly limited opportunity for the poor to improve their lot dwindles even more every day. Even pre-COVID, the world was looking more and more like a dystopian sci-fi movie, and I'm going to be the asshole who shows up with a newborn to drain even more resources? Nah.

Beyond all that, I also know me. I can stay sober, I can make all the spiritual progress in the world, but at my core, I will always be a self-centered egomaniac. I am too busy being a kid to take care of a kid. I know a lot of people feel that way right up to the moment when they become a parent, but I just don't want that responsibility. I know for a guy who is nearly fifty that is kind of pathetic, but the bottom line is I like my life as it is. I respect the idea of parenting and I respect kids themselves too much to simply roll the dice and say "Fuck it!" on this one. Ultimately, I think not having kids is about the most responsible decision I've ever made.

It's strange to me that, in life, once you reach a certain age, the default mode is to have children, and those of us who choose not to are forever explaining our reasoning, then having that reasoning psychologically dissected by everyone else. For a decision as big and consequential as this, doesn't it make more sense that those who choose to have kids should be the ones having to justify their choice? Don't get me wrong: There are plenty of good, ethical, loving reasons to have kids, and the perpetuation of the human race does require at least some of us to do so. But there are plenty of willing volunteers for that. They don't need me.

As much as I've been pretending this is a self-help book, this is one place where I'm not suggesting there is any great wisdom in my personal beliefs. On the contrary. I just want you to understand my position. If you really want to give up all your freedoms to deal with crying babies, dirty diapers, and the soul-depleting, bankruptcy-inducing cost of an increasingly ornamental college degree, have at it, dude!

I had a conversation with my friend Abdalla a few years ago. Abdalla is an amazingly smart and spiritually enlightened guy I went to high school with in London. Now he's a doctor and has five kids. I explained all my reasoning for not having kids to him and told him I didn't want to bring someone into a world who would have to suffer, who wouldn't have the opportunities that were available to me or to my parents' generation. He asked me a question: "With all the poverty, famine, and disease in Africa, do you think people there are less happy?" My knee-jerk reaction was "Yes, of course they are." But he made a compelling case that on an individual level, he didn't think they were. Without a doubt, having money, having resources, can make life more comfortable. But happiness and comfort aren't the same thing. Happiness is really a measure of someone's capacity to love other people and to receive love, to feel that human connection. If anything, money is a barrier to that, not a conduit.

It was an interesting point, and I could see how it was convincing for Abdalla himself, but not for me. Ultimately, even if I was to have a more optimistic view of humanity, if I was to grant that a child born into dire circumstances could have a reasonable chance at happiness, that wouldn't change the things I know about me. I don't think I can handle the emotional burden of reproducing, so I'm not doing it. I figure I'm better serving humanity by getting a vasectomy. I'm sure lots of people who have seen my body of work would agree.

Once I made that decision, I was excited to make this vasectomy an *event*. First, before I scheduled the operation, it seemed worthwhile to see if I even *needed* it. I mean, I've put my poor testicles through a lot. For many years, I received more than my fair share of hard kicks to the nuts, and I stapled my balls to my leg regularly—for years, it was a go-to move onstage, during interviews, and wherever else the impulse hit me. With all the trauma they've been through, it was possible that I'd been firing blanks for years. So I went to a fertility clinic, cranked out a load, and they put it under a microscope. A regular healthy load would have 20 million sperm per milliliter of jizz. Mine had 51 million, which I guess only proves that whatever doesn't kill you makes you stronger. The vasectomy was a go.

I decided to get it done in Puerto Rico as a way to help promote the spaying and neutering of pets down there after a hurricane in 2018. I flew there with Chris Pontius, Scott Randolph, and Lux, and we filmed the whole trip, including the surgery. The doctor warned me not to take any shots to the nuts in the next few days, but that of course was the whole point.

The Olympiad began before I was even out of the medical clinic. I performed my classic "double-back" trick for the doctor, whipping my cock and balls back and forth and then catching them between my thighs in a "mangina" pose. He loved it, though all the people staring from the waiting room were a little less amused. That was just the beginning, though.

At the animal clinic where they were spaying and neutering pets, I arranged to ride a horse, bareback, around a track while still in my hospital gown. At first, it was just a slow trot, with Scott holding the horse's tether. But soon enough, the horse took off in a full gallop, Scott couldn't keep up, and my balls were getting smashed every step of the way. I could not fall off that fucking horse fast enough.

Next on the Olympic slate, Pontius jumped on my lap to pop a balloon, which fucking hurt. Then he hung me upside down like a piñata, so local kids could swing at my nuts with a bat. Some of these so-called kids were more like teenagers, and they were not going easy on my nads. The following day, I went flyboarding. At the end of the Olympiad, my nuts were purple, bruised, swollen, and, frankly, kind of gross. I couldn't have been more thrilled with the footage of my ball sack in such a state—the whole bit we filmed really paid off. Six weeks later, I returned to the fertility clinic, cranked out another load, and confirmed that the vasectomy had done its job: There would be no miniature Steve-Os running around, defiling themselves for the amusement of future generations.

The Vasectomy Olympics became one of the core set pieces in my Bucket List tour, and when I would show the footage of the actual vasectomy, big burly dudes in the audience would frequently straight up faint. I don't know if that says more about man's primal instinct to reproduce or about how on point that old joke about macho dudes and vasectomies really was.

*   *   *

As much as that vasectomy was a renunciation of my obligation to leave a legacy behind, the whole concept of a legacy is a tough nut to crack, no pun intended. Swearing off any thoughts about what future generations will think of you can veer dangerously close to being a nihilistic asshole. *Fuck it, I'll pollute the world, I'll hoover up all its resources, because I'm not going to be around to have to deal with the fallout.* None of us should want to be that prick.

Besides, while there is an inherent logic to not caring about your legacy, since you won't be around to experience it, I can't ignore my impulse to care inordinately about what everyone else is saying about me, *especially* when I'm not around to hear it. Since I can't wrap my head around the conundrum of nonexistence, the only way for me to think about it is to imagine my death as the ultimate opportunity for people to talk behind my back. So what will they be saying? That I was a dickhead? That I made them laugh? That I led an epic life? That beneath all the blood, fire, sperm, and bravado, I was actually a good person?

There is a strong argument to be made that the real legacy we leave behind, the way we really live forever, is in the memories of the people we touch during our lives, and the impact we make on them. As much as I hope that all my video footage will keep reminding people of who I was, in all likelihood, I'm not going to be Harry Houdini or P. T. Barnum. In one hundred years, no one is going to be making a musical about my life starring Hugh Jackman (or Hugh Jackman's great-great-grandson). My friends, my family, they'll think about me and talk about me for a while. I imagine for at least a couple of generations, stories of "crazy Uncle Steve" will get passed down. Then, one day, that will end. But the ways we affect people, the ways we shape others, that keeps rippling on through time. Ideals, beliefs, love, trauma—all that is quietly transferred to each successive generation whether we want it to be or not. I guess what I'm saying is that in two hundred and fifty years, when some dude is shooting fireworks out of his butthole or setting his hair on fire or jerking off as he jumps out of an airplane, even though he might not know my name, a part of me will be alive in him.

11

When the World Is Going to Hell, It Helps if You've Already Been There

I try hard to be an optimistic guy, and in the small universe I've created around me, there's plenty to be optimistic about. But if I take a step back and look at the rest of the world, the picture looks grim. I am quite certain you didn't pick up this book to hear a reasoned analysis of the dire ecological, socioeconomic, and geopolitical challenges the world is facing from a guy who once played tetherball with a beehive, but suffice to say, I think humanity is pretty fucked at this point. Here's the good news, though: The human race is almost certain to survive your life and probably the lives of everyone you love. Beyond that, I can make no guarantees.

As I'm writing this, we're well into year two of a global pandemic, so predicting that the End Times are around the corner feels less out-there than it once did. But just to be clear—I was into this apocalyptic shit way before it was cool.

In the days when I was largely subsisting on a diet of nitrous oxide, ketamine, cocaine, and booze, I was also, coincidentally enough, prone to batshit insane thoughts and conspiracies, many of which involved aliens and most of which revolved around the end of the world. If you were promoting any sort of crackpot apocalyptic spirituality on the internet around 2007, there's a good chance I took a deep dive into it and then spewed it back out as barely intelligible gibberish to hundreds of people on my Rad Email List.

What, you may ask, was my Rad Email List? Oof. In a strictly technical sense, it could be considered social media before the term "social media" had been popularized. I had compiled a list of a couple hundred email addresses of celebrities, lawyers, agents, managers, producers, studio executives, journalists, and the like, who all had one thing in common: Each of them had at some point been foolish enough to share their personal email address with me. I would regularly blast out arrogant, rambling, incoherent messages to this list on any and all topics—the more inappropriate, the better. There is almost nothing that filled me with more shame in the early days of my sobriety than the horseshit I was regularly disseminating on my Rad Email List.

One of my favorite subjects back then—for Rad Emails, for my dumbass (and mercifully aborted) rap album, and for wild-eyed, in-person rants—was the end of the world. I was regularly on multiday no-sleep drug binges, and I'd spend those sleepless days glued to my computer doing internet "research" on other-dimensional spiritual entities that were utterly fascinated with the human race and, in many cases, directly involved with its coming annihilation. You see, when I was able to ingest just the right amount of drugs (or sometimes more than the right amount), I believed I was in direct communication with many of these entities, so I had credible knowledge that some of them were actively trying to rescue us, while others were trying to destroy us. So, yeah, I was in deep. But my Armageddon fetish didn't necessarily require extraterrestrial invasions. You may remember that there were a lot of people who were subscribed to a supposed Mayan prophecy that the world was going to end on December 21, 2012. I was all in on that shit too.

Although the drugs absolutely accelerated and enhanced this kind of lunacy, even in sobriety I have not been immune to this sort of thinking. If I'm being honest, to this day I retain a soft spot in my heart for anyone who has a whacked-out conviction that the world is speeding toward imminent oblivion and an entertaining story about how it's going to get there. After the 2008 financial crisis, it seemed like there were more and more of those people around, or at least around me.

My dad, a retired corporate executive who has always been a voice of reason in my life, started sounding the alarm to me around 2011 or so. He wasn't spewing nonsense about aliens and Mayans. He had hard facts and reasoned prognostications. The U.S. economy was an elaborate Ponzi scheme that eventually would crash, Dad told me. He rolled out statistics that sounded ominous: At that time, the national debt was *merely* $13 trillion, but when you kicked in unfunded obligations for Medicare, Medicaid, and Social Security, plus the debt racked up by state and local governments, the true figure was closer to $100 trillion. That's a lot of fucking money. To pay that off with tax increases and spending cuts was politically impossible, so the only way out was to reduce the value of the debt by promoting inflation.

In other words, they would have to devalue the dollar until it was nearly worthless. According to Dad, once that happened, the American system as we know it would crumble. The dollar would completely collapse. The ripple effects would be shocking. Government programs and pensions would go unfunded. Public employees would go unpaid. Shelves in the grocery store would be bare. Rioting and looting would be commonplace. Our current democracy would give way to some form of military government.

The big takeaway was: prepare yourself. Dad encouraged me to control my spending, avoid debt, accumulate savings, and invest in gold and other precious metals. This more-than-slightly paranoid worldview dovetailed pretty dangerously with my pre-existing midlife fears that I was destined to lose everything I'd spent my life working for, so I took notice and did as advised.

Around this same time, I was flying to Europe for my first ever stand-up dates there. The guy sitting next to me was reading a book called *Emergency: This Book Will Save Your Life*. It was by Neil Strauss, who had written the Mötley Crüe book *The Dirt*, which gave the author instant cred in my eyes. This new book was about what to do in the case of an end-of-the-world-as-we-know-it-type disaster, which was, again, totally in my wheelhouse. To write it, Strauss had embedded himself in the world of doomsday preppers. Considering that I was already jazzed for the coming apocalypse, the book became a bit of a guide for me.

I found other books and websites too. The deeper I sunk into prepper literature, the more real my plans became. I started stashing gold coins in foreign bank vaults, hoarding five-gallon water jugs, scouting for off-the-grid locations to bunker down during this coming reckoning, and just generally building my doomsday bugout plan. Although 2012 came and went without the world ending, the signs were all still flashing bright red, indicating societal breakdown was on the horizon. In fact, they still are.

*   *   *

There's something about living in California that makes doomsday feel imminent. The juxtaposition of the obnoxious displays of extreme wealth and the equally visible homelessness and poverty, all against the backdrop of wildfires literally burning towns off the map, can put you in a mood. Don't get me wrong, I love Hollywood and I love living here even more. Despite that, I'm just patiently waiting for it to burn to the ground.

A few years ago, Scott and I drove up to San Francisco for a long weekend of shows and surfing. On Saturday, around noon, we went for lunch at a vegetarian restaurant in the Tenderloin district. We had what I call my "super pack" in the car, which is basically a fully functional studio in a backpack that includes a laptop, a high-end camera, multiple lenses, and an iPad. We parked the car right across the street, and then sat at a table by the window where we could see it. When we came back to the car after lunch, the window was busted out and the super pack was gone, along with an iPhone, some wetsuits, a skateboard, and $3,000 in cash from the merch we had sold so far that weekend. For whoever took it, I'd venture to guess that was the single most lucrative smash-and-grab they'd ever undertaken. The fact that the break-in had occurred in broad daylight on a busy street, while Scott and I ostensibly were watching, speaks both to the desperation (and talent) of the perpetrator(s), as well as just how unsurprising it must have been to anyone who might have witnessed it.

When we went to the police station to report the incident, the cops literally laughed at us. They didn't even pretend that they were going to investigate. This kind of theft was so common in San Francisco that they seemed to regard it as barely even against the law anymore. As we relayed this story to other people throughout the rest of that weekend, the responses were pretty uniform: "Same exact thing happened to me."

If California seemed to be teetering close to the brink, I viewed San Francisco as the canary in the coal mine for the whole country. The tech economy had exacerbated the wealth gap in the city. Gentrification and sky-high real-estate prices had made it so working people couldn't afford to live anywhere near where their jobs were. Homelessness was endemic. Burglaries and robberies were commonplace. It was really just an amped-up version of what was happening all over the country.

If you scratch beneath the surface level of many of the major political movements in the United States over the past decade and a half—Occupy Wall Street, MAGA, Bernie Bros, Black Lives Matter—they're all fueled by a similar base anger. The poor are getting poorer, and they are—absolutely appropriately—fucking pissed. The root of nearly every problem on earth is human greed. It's the age-old story of the haves versus the have-nots. The haves have long pitted different groups of have-nots against each other, but eventually the have-nots are going to get wise to this shit. Soon after that, they'll be at the castle gates with proverbial torches and pitchforks. Or actual torches and pitchforks.

When wealthy people campaign for lower taxes and cutting social programs, they're making a risky calculation that they can build their castle walls high enough to keep these have-nots at bay long enough to make it somebody else's problem. The way I think about it, it's very much in the interest of the haves to address this wealth disparity before it impacts their personal safety. I mean, I didn't expect voting for Joe Biden to be in my short-term financial self-interest, but longer term, I believed that to be our best chance for having fewer homeless people and allowing more sick people to access medical care. I'm well aware that voicing a political opinion is a losing proposition for anyone these days, even more so for a guy who once snorted an earthworm up his nose, but let me just say that if the wealth gap shrunk, if there was less crime, I'd be a lot fucking happier. I'd rather have far less in savings but *feel* safe in my home.

As much as I'd like to do my part to help end that widening inequality and as much as I am trying to, there is a selfish part of me that also just wants to disappear. It's not just a fear of being that man in the high castle with the pitchfork brigade at my gate; it's that seeing grinding poverty all the time, up close, and feeling relatively powerless to change it, is a fucking bummer. I know, I know, it's not nearly as much of a bummer to be the rich asshole living *near* poverty as it is to be the guy having to live *in* it, but it's a bummer nonetheless. I can't help but feel like there's a reckoning coming, and I don't want to be around when it arrives.

*　　*　　*

Disaster prepping is quite the rabbit hole to disappear down, and it's not necessarily one that I'm recommending you dive into with every ounce of your being. Some people make it an all-encompassing lifestyle. For me, it's been more of a hobby. See, the one secret about all this doomsday prep that no one really talks about but which I want to share with you is that it's a lot of fucking fun. Sure, you can get wrapped up in all the paranoia and the insanity, but browsing for survival gadgets, searching for a place to escape to, imagining how you're going to get there, how you'll survive once you're there? All that is like a bizarro-world fantasy role-playing game. What kind of water purification system will you install at your off-the-grid retreat? What about solar power? How will you handle security?

There's something strange in the human psyche that gets excited at the prospect of incoming societal disaster. Or maybe it's only douchebags like me—people who are better equipped with resources to weather a hurricane or a civil war or a zombie invasion—that get a little giddy whenever they hear those beeps from the emergency broadcast system. But I think most people's brains start pumping adrenaline as part of a fight-or-flight survival mechanism, which makes the whole experience of imagining and planning that fight or flight a little thrilling.

One thing I learned quickly about a bugout plan is that it's all well and good to have a super-secure off-the-grid destination to ride out whatever you need to ride out, but when the shit goes down and disaster strikes, you need a reliable way to get there fast. The freeways will likely be gridlocked, and if you're sitting in traffic, you're a sitting duck for whatever you're running from. For the megarich, the answer is probably a helicopter or a private plane that will ferry you to your mountain bunker, but that's not really me. For preppers on a budget, if you need to get your ass out of town fast, the best option is a motorcycle, because you can split lanes to cruise through traffic.

Once I discovered that, I was all about it. The only problem was I didn't know how to ride a motorcycle, so I signed up for a three-day intensive motorcycle school. Day one was in a classroom, essentially learning the basics about motorcycles. It went fine. On the second day, we met in a parking lot to start riding. That's where it began to unravel for me. I was confused by how to operate the clutch—I've still never learned to drive a stick shift, and I'm sure I never will—and given how many accidents aren't even the fault of the motor-cycle driver, having anything slow down my reaction time when I'm already the worst driver on the road didn't make much sense to me. I mean, there's no point in surviving the apocalypse only to get killed because you suck at riding a motorcycle, right? Also, remem-ber Elisabetta, George Clooney's supermodel ex-girlfriend? I'd just met her at that time, and she invited me to come over to her place on what happened to be the second day of motorcycle school. I never made it to day three. Ultimately, my desire to crawl into bed with this gorgeous Italian model outweighed my fear of the world ending. I became a motorcycle school dropout.

Despite that failure, it didn't slow down my search for a bugout destination. For years, I have been scouting for poten-tial locations to plant the fortress of solitude that I'll retreat to when I finally decide to pull the rip cord on this get-the-fuck-out-of-Dodge plan. The search itself has been so much fun that I wonder if I've subconsciously prolonged it because I don't want it to end. In fact, it continues to this day.

A lot of my surf trips have involved evaluating various

countries as potential places to disappear to. Since getting together with Lux, my idea is that this destination could combine two of my obsessions: It will be both a future getaway and the home for the animal sanctuary that Lux and I have been dreaming about.

Originally, Lux and I envisioned the sanctuary as a tourist destination, with a bed-and-breakfast, a Steve-O museum of foolishness, and maybe even a makeshift amusement park, all of which would raise money to help support the sanctuary. But over the last couple of years, as I've started to think about it as part of this bugout plan, I've decided that I don't want anyone to know where the fuck we are. I want the place to be an off-the-map, self-sustaining compound, where we grow our own food, generate our own energy, take care of our half-assed Noah's ark family of rescue animals, and hide out from the worldwide zombie apocalypse.

I know all that sounds fucking crazy, but as I told you earlier in this book, I don't go halfway on anything. I mean, granted, it will take quite the feat of self-restraint for a guy who has spent his whole life begging for attention to suddenly disappear to a secret lair and crave privacy. But maybe I can somehow have my cake and eat it too by turning my disappearing act into a public spectacle. Maybe I can gin up the drama and have tabloids speculating on "Where's Steve-O?" I can surreptitiously feed my beloved TMZ a steady diet of clues. I have a sneaking suspicion that I would be quite happy with the life of a famous recluse like Howard Hughes, Richard Simmons, or the Unabomber.

None of this is meant to be prescriptive. I'm not suggesting you start subscribing to end-times conspiracy theories or building a bunker in your backyard or hoarding canned goods and firearms. I mean, go ahead if that's your thing, but I don't think that's the part that will really help you if and when everything falls apart. What is useful to almost everyone, though, is to think hard about what you *really* need in your life, to assess who your real friends are, to strip all the extraneous shit out, and to figure out what you can't do without. Thinking about all this end-of-days shit does exactly that. It focuses your mind on what's important to you. Even if the zombies don't rise up and turn the world into an apocalyptic hellscape, that's good information to know.

All this provides some necessary context for the closest most of us have come to an actual apocalyptic hellscape, the COVID-19 pandemic. Granted, it's been a pretty peculiar hellscape, one in which a not-insignificant percentage of the population and their political representatives have consistently argued for their freedom to make this hellscape more hellish, but anyone who knows anything about zombie films knows that it's not the zombies that do most of the damage. It's the humans.

*   *   *

In early 2020, things were looking pretty sweet in my world. I'd been on my Bucket List stand-up tour, and we were selling out shows well in advance of my arrival in most cities. In early March, I got the call from my agent that I had been hoping to get for quite some time. He told me that my stand-up shows had gotten too big for comedy clubs, so it was going to be all theaters for me from here on out. If you can fill theaters, the financial model improves considerably and the workload becomes more manageable too. But more than that, it just felt like a real graduation moment, an acknowledgment of the hard work I'd put in over the previous ten years. I'd made a long bet on myself that I could pull off a career in stand-up. Not many people would've backed that bet, but it had worked.

When I got that big call, I was on the set of *Jackass Forever*. I had finally worked out all the contract bullshit with *Jackass* producers and I was with my bros filming material for the fourth movie. Paramount had seen some of the early footage, and they were so psyched on it that, several weeks later, they decided *Jackass 4* would open on the weekend of July Fourth, 2021, which is the biggest movie weekend of the summer. Our previous films had all premiered at the top of the box office charts, but after more than a decade away—a decade during which YouTube and social media had made stunts and pranks ubiquitous in people's lives—there was some nervousness as to whether audiences would still be there for us. That release date decision was a huge vote of confidence.

I'd also just recorded the first few episodes of a new podcast, *Wild Ride! with Steve-O*, in a van I'd had customized for podcasting. I was so stoked on this van. It enabled me to cruise right up to a guest's house and start recording. The first couple interviews I did in that van, with Tony Hawk and Bert Kreischer, had gone great, and I was already planning more. Everything seemed to be coming up Steve-O in 2020.

Then came COVID. As everyone probably remembers, over the course of just a few days in mid-March, the whole world ground to a halt. Life was pretty much canceled. We were all told to shelter in place in our homes and keep our distance from other people until further notice. The seriousness of the situation washed over me quickly. My first thought was *Man, I can't believe all this is happening to me!* I'd finally graduated to playing theaters and now there would be no touring at all for the foreseeable future. *Jackass 4* was poised to be a huge, blockbuster film, but who knew when people would ever actually go back to sitting side by side with strangers in a crowded movie theater. The future for big cinema chains like AMC and Regal looked fucking bleak. And as for the podcast and the van that I'd tricked out for it, no one wanted to sit in a fucking van with me for an hour anymore. I was getting royally fucked by COVID!

Don't think I don't know how absurd it is to think that *I* was the main victim of this global pandemic, particularly considering I hadn't even gotten sick. But hey, narcissism is no joke. Growing up may have made me more aware that I'm a shameless attention whore, but it hasn't stopped me from being one.

I later came to my senses. Well, a little. I remember having a conversation a few months later with Eric André on my podcast, which I'd continued to do virtually. Eric had been working on this movie called *Bad Trip* for a long time. It was produced by Jeff Tremaine and had a similar concept to *Bad Grandpa*, a narrative film driven by hidden-camera footage of real people and pranks. This was a labor of love for Eric that was finally coming to fruition. The studio had spent a bunch of money on advertising and promotion. There was a great trailer and some commercials already running. Then a week before the movie was set to debut at a film festival, COVID shut everything down. He was devastated. On this podcast, I told Eric that no one had been fucked over more by COVID than Mötley Crüe—who had already booked a stadium tour—and Eric André. He nodded a little and then deadpanned, "There are also people dying and stuff."

Oh right, yeah. Reality check: Maybe a few people have had it worse.

I think it took us all a while to get our bearings in the pandemic, but once I did, I realized that I was uniquely positioned to thrive in the worldwide shutdown. All my doomsday prepping—not to mention the podcasting RV conversion van that allowed me to shelter in place pretty much anyplace I felt like it—left me pretty well suited for quarantine.

Far from fucking me over, the pandemic ended up being one of the best things that ever happened to me, or at least to my career. It forced me to quit touring and to concentrate on building other parts of my business. For as much as I complain about the grind of touring, I don't know if I ever would've been able to step away from the guaranteed money it was bringing in.

Once there were no shows, that crutch of touring income was gone. I had been working very hard to post tons of content on social media for quite a few years, but I wasn't really working very smartly. I would look at these other online personalities—people like David Dobrik or Logan Paul or the Nelk Boys—and just get all kinds of frustrated that they were getting so much more traction and making so much more money doing essentially the same kinds of things I was doing. The more I studied it, the more I started to understand how various pieces of content could work to enhance each other. Previously, my strategy had been to splatter shit all over the place and just hope that something resonated. Now I was learning to be more strategic. I felt like I was cracking the code.

As an example, I set up the paywall on my website to start selling my *Gnarly* comedy special. I then used videos on YouTube, Facebook, and Instagram to drive interest toward that special. So, while those videos could earn revenue on their own, they were also promoting the special. Merch sales, which used to primarily happen on tour, picked up dramatically online too. YouTube and social media posts could help push people toward the online merch store. After doing a handful of charity fundraising initiatives, which generally involved selling autographed 8x10 photos for various causes during the pandemic, we discovered that the fulfillment company doing all our shipping was one of the biggest benefactors of our charitable efforts. My merch operation had become such a big piece of my business that we decided to move the whole operation in-house. I rented a warehouse and created a fulfillment center business, cleverly named Tight Box Packing. I also used social media to push the podcast, which really began to take off.

Doing the podcast has been a real education, and not just business-wise. It's forced me to listen to how I sound when I talk to people. And, man, for as much of a self-centered asshole as I have always known myself to be, it was painful to hear just how bad it could be.

Initially, I was pretty oblivious to all this. After I recorded that first podcast with Tony Hawk, I was so happy with how well it seemed to go that I immediately sent it to this guy who works in podcast production. I told him I couldn't have imagined it going any better. He wasn't nearly as impressed with me as I was with myself.

"You've got this legendary icon in your van and you're not even letting him speak," he told me. I went back and watched it, and he was right. I was sucking up every ounce of oxygen in that fucking van. It was mortifying to witness. It made me self-conscious, in a good way, as I interviewed more people. I started noticing my conversational tics, the main one being that I have a tendency to want to share so much about myself and whatever brilliant fucking thing I'm thinking about at that moment that I tend to let that impulse overpower everything else. I needed to shut the fuck up, let other people talk, and concentrate on listening to what they were actually saying.

I know this seems like a really fucking basic rule of communication to finally be learning in my mid-forties, but hey, what can I say? I'm slow. Podcasting has turned into an exercise in addressing a pretty critical deficiency in my communication skills.

Not everyone is as self-obsessed as me, but I think a lot of people don't fully realize what they sound like when they talk to other people. As a remedy for this, I was thinking that I'd recommend that everyone start their own podcast, but I think that's already happened. For the few of you out there who are not yet hosting your own podcast, though, I genuinely think there's a tremendous value in recording yourself during normal conversations and listening back to what you sound like. A lot of people cringe at hearing their own voice, but I think it's less the voice than what it's saying. I know our thoughts always sound brilliant in our heads, but when they come stumbling out of our mouths, they have a tendency to sound, well, a lot less graceful and insightful than we had hoped. The more you hear it, the more you have a chance to adjust it and finally become the person that you are in your head.

For as much as 2020 sucked for so many people, I'm almost ashamed to admit it was one of the best years of my life. From a business standpoint, I not only made more money than I'd ever made, but I set up my business to be more integrated, strategic, and gratifying in the future. On a personal level, stripping my life down to its bare essentials was both clarifying and fulfilling. Having the people who were important to me pulled even closer didn't rattle any of those relationships—it made them stronger. This was particularly the case with Lux. So many news stories during the pandemic pointed out how difficult it had been on relationships. As husbands and wives were suddenly thrown together in an enclosed space for months at a time, many of them realized they couldn't stand each other. With Lux and me, it was the opposite. I'd wanted to find someone who'd be there for me when the shit hit the fan, and now that it has, the hard work we'd put into the relationship feels like it's paying off. Being together 24-7 made us all the more certain that that's the way we want to spend the rest of our lives.

Of course, having such a kickass year during a time when most of the world is suffering is kind of a weird one. It's hard not to feel like a shithead yammering on about how much money I'm making and how fucking excellent my life is when so many others are sick or dying or alone or struggling to make ends meet. I understand if reading about my pandemic triumphs makes you want to beat the shit out of me. That's totally fair. Just understand that for however well I might be doing at the moment, however much I'm crowing about my wonderful career, or my beautiful relationship, none of that has appreciably fixed all the broken bits inside of me. As you well know if you've already read this far in the book, I'm still a fucking mess. So that should make you feel better.

A lot of people have asked me whether the anxiety and stress of the pandemic have put my sobriety at risk, and the honest truth is that they haven't. In fact, I have been almost alarmingly laid back about the pandemic, from the beginning. I've largely done what medical professionals advise to keep myself and others healthy. But what I haven't done is freak the fuck out about any of it. It's hard to know exactly why that is, but I do believe that the hell that I have put myself (and others) through with my various addictions and obsessions over the years has helped to make this hell more endurable. I've put myself under enormous stress in the past and faced some hard truths—about who I am, what I want, and what's important to me. I've stared into the void and learned to deal with what I saw staring back at me.

I wouldn't recommend addiction to anyone, but the process of recovery has things in it that are valuable for all of us. It breaks you down and builds you back up stronger. In fact, addiction is the only disease that can make you into an improved version of yourself once you treat it. With any other disease, you can only hope to get back to as good as you already were before. By that measure, I consider addicts and alcoholics in recovery to be the luckiest people of all.

When you get sober, the serenity prayer is drilled into you pretty hard, and a lot of emphasis is placed on not spinning out over things you can't control. This pandemic has offered an extreme exercise in dealing with shit that is totally out of your control, so I'm damn glad that I've had practice with that.

12

Don't Be a Selfish Dick

Are you happy?

I know that sounds like a simple question, but to me, it's super fucked-up. The question itself makes me incredibly uncomfortable. When someone asks me that, it feels almost like an accusation. I get defensive. I mean, what does it mean to be happy? Am I content? Am I killing it in my career? Are the people I love healthy? Do I feel good about myself? Do the answers to all these questions need to be yes for me to be happy? Should happiness even be the goal?

The entire idea of happiness makes me spin out, so let me just put that question to the side for a second and tell you a story.

In 2009, I was a contestant on *Dancing with the Stars*. At the time, I had been sober for less than a year. It was my first professional appearance since melting down and landing in the psych ward. I had always struggled to be comfortable in my own skin, and now I was going on prime-time national television and doing something I sucked at—dancing—to earn something I had always yearned for—public affirmation. Sure, I was no stranger to crappy performances on television, but they were always *supposed* to be crappy. In this case, sucking was a bad thing, plus it came with criticism and a humiliating elimination.

None of it felt good or healthy. I was emotionally fraying and uncomfortable all the time. It was too fucking much. I felt like I might fall off the wagon. So I did what I was supposed to do and called a mentor of mine in recovery. I told him I was not okay, and he listened.

"That's fine," he said. "You're not supposed to feel good all the time. Sometimes you're not going to be okay. Sometimes you're going to feel like shit." He let that all sink in and then he continued. "The one thing you can always do when you're feeling bad that will make you feel better is to conduct yourself like a gentleman. If you act like a decent human being, you're giving yourself something to feel good about. You can be proud that no matter how bad you feel, you tried to do the right thing. That's not nothing."

It helped to hear that, but it took a minute for it to fully sink in. If happiness means feeling good all the time or even most of the time, then that is an unfair target, not just for me, but for all of us. Controlling how you're feeling on a day-to-day basis is impossible. But what is actually doable is to control the way you act. I've spent a lot of this book trying to draw some sort of wisdom from my crazy life, but if I got loads of it wrong, or if it was all just too much to remember, the best I can do to boil it down is this: just don't be a selfish dick. That's kind of my version of the Golden Rule. If you can avoid being a selfish dick, it may not make you happy, but it will give you something tangible to feel good about. At least you'll be moving in the right direction.

Pretty much everything is improved by thinking about others before you think about yourself. But however simple this rule is to explain, it's hands down the hardest to follow. I still fail at it *all the time*. Selfishness is literally embedded in our DNA. In my DNA, it seems to be on steroids. Our genes want us to take care of ourselves so they can be passed on to the next generation. That's just science. The fact that we're all hardwired to be *selfish*, yet the path to feeling good, to something approaching happiness, is to act *selflessly* is the kind of existential paradox that will either make you laugh or make you crazy. Maybe both.

*   *   *

In 2017, I got a call from Jukka Hildén. Jukka is a Finnish guy who had a *Jackass*-like stunt show called *The Dudesons*. They made a version of it for MTV in 2010 with Knoxville and Tremaine's production company, Dickhouse, and I had hung out with Jukka before, so I was sort of friendly with him. When he called me in 2017, he was doing something entirely different. He had his own production company that had made this mountain climbing reality show back in Finland. Now they were going to re-create it for the U.S. market. It was called *Ultimate Expedition* and the gist of the show was straightforward: a bunch of celebrities climb a mountain in the Peruvian Andes. Jukka wanted me to do it.

I should say, right off the bat, I had no interest in doing this show. Mountain climbing is not exactly my thing, and I was pretty sure I wasn't going to look cool doing it. Maybe more important, post–*Dancing with the Stars*, my feeling about being a contestant on reality shows is that it's generally an awful look. If you're a celebrity with nothing better to do than participate in that sort of thing, it seems to me like you're hurting for money or attention or both. I have occasionally ignored this feeling for various reasons, which include that free ski vacation in Austria for British television, but this didn't feel like a good candidate for an exception. The series was going to be shown on YouTube Red, which is what YouTube was calling its premium paid subscription platform at that moment. It was part of an experiment YouTube was doing to see if they could compete with the Netflixes of the world. When I considered it logically, there was no good reason for me to say yes to Jukka.

But I did. Why? Well, when Jukka was doing *The Dudesons* series with Dickhouse, he had reached out to ask me to appear on an episode. The show was new to American audiences and any appearances from the guys from *Jackass*, any nods of approval from us, would go a long way toward bringing our fans to the show. But at the time, I felt threatened by *The Dudesons*. I didn't like that Tremaine was making a show that was kind of like *Jackass* but wasn't *Jackass*. It seemed like these Finnish dudes were horning in on our idea and on our fans, even though I knew they had actually been filming stunts and pranks in Finland since before *Jackass* existed. I worried that they were working to undermine the *Jackass* brand. So I refused to appear on *The Dudesons*. In fact, I didn't really even refuse. I simply didn't return his calls. And that made me feel like a selfish fucking dick.

I wanted to make it up to Jukka, so I explained to him that even though I felt like it didn't make much sense for my career,

I would do the Peru show because I felt bad that I'd hung him out to dry on *The Dudesons*. I wanted to make amends. It turns out, Jukka hadn't been holding any grudge against me. In fact, he hadn't been aware of any tension between us at all, but, nonetheless, I felt good about my decision. It later occurred to me that climbing a twenty-thousand-foot mountain in order to remedy a barely perceptible professional slight is the very definition of the punishment not fitting the crime, but as I mentioned before, moderation isn't my thing.

The show was a fucking nightmare. Nearly all the rest of the cast were YouTube stars. Except for me and Chuck Liddell, a retired UFC fighter, no one else really had much of a public profile off the platform. The pay was rather meager too, especially considering the job meant being off the grid entirely for three weeks. Every cast member was also required to post an obnoxious number of videos to their YouTube channels to promote the show. I still have no idea how I agreed to that one. Worse than all that, you may not know this, but climbing mountains is really fucking hard. Not totally unlike *Dancing with the Stars*, I did not feel comfortable being filmed doing something I was terrible at.

Filming that show was a strange experience. In addition to the main production crew, each contestant was filming themselves for all those contractually obligated videos we were required to post. The idea was that our videos would drive traffic to the show, and that the show would in turn drive viewers to our channels. I had to create two videos to post during each of the ten weeks the show would run. If math isn't your strong suit, that's *twenty* fucking videos.

The whole setup was a strange inversion of what a production set usually is. Normally, if anyone pulls out a camera while the production's cameras are rolling, that person will be in deep-ass shit, because they don't want you cannibalizing their content. Here, that was the whole point. We were supposed to turn in all of our own footage every day so the producers could sift through it and potentially use it for the main show. That didn't sit well with me at all. As I mentioned before, I slave over the stuff I post on YouTube. I want my videos to be the greatest shit I can possibly make. Having to post twenty videos from this expedition was already utterly ridiculous, but now these producers were going to help themselves to my best footage? Fuck that!

I was constantly arguing and complaining about all this stuff, feeling completely stressed out over it, all while I was living outdoors in a tent and climbing a fucking mountain. It was completely predictable that under these circumstances, each of the cast members would reach their breaking point, and I think all of us did. I know I reached mine, over and over and over. I was constantly having tantrums, which was not a good look for me. I was blowing up at people, then apologizing to them, then blowing up again, then apologizing some more. To make matters worse, when the final show came out, I feel like they did me dirty in the edit. There was plenty of available footage to make me look like a shithead, and the producers did just that, but without much in the way of context. I felt used.

In the end, the whole experience seemed like another one to file under "no good deed goes unpunished." To this day, though, I can't say I regret it at all. My intentions were selfless, and I could keep falling back on that same thing I was told during *Dancing with the Stars*: Do the right thing, and even though it might not make you happy, it will give you something to *feel* good about. For all my problems and tantrums, I hadn't been a selfish dick. At least not *all* the time.

Even though the trip sucked dick, there was some tangible good that came out of it. The final night I was in Peru, there was a big party. Since I don't drink, I stayed for less than thirty minutes, then went back to the hotel and went to sleep. Late that night, a guy named Paul Brisske, who was in charge of digital production on the show, made his way up onto the roof of a nightclub by himself and then fell three stories into a fenced-off construction site next door. He broke six ribs in nine places, punctured both his lungs (fortunately only one of them collapsed), shattered his wrist, and snapped both his left arm and leg. He laid there among all this rubble, unable to move, until four p.m. the following day, when someone finally discovered him. I didn't even find out about this accident until weeks later, and he was still in the hospital at that point. I sent him a text to congratulate him on being a *way* gnarlier dude than I would ever be. A few months later, Paul left Jukka's production company and reached out to me to ask if I needed any help with producing or editing my content. I immediately hired him. Paul is amazing with video and has been a huge part of transforming and professionalizing my operation, not to mention a great fucking friend.

He was not the only stray that I picked up in Peru. I also found a dog on the streets who began following me around. There were tons of street dogs there, and I was on the prowl for one to keep me company at our base camp during the expedition, but most of them wanted nothing to do with me. Except for this one. I fed her, and she started trailing me all over the place. I named her Wendy. At one point, I had to go into a building that wouldn't allow dogs inside, so I figured that would be the last I'd see of Wendy. But when I came out of a restaurant later that night, there she was, surrounded by a crew of other friendly street dogs. It's as if she vouched for me to them. Eventually we walked back across town to the hotel, and Wendy followed me the whole way. I snuck her inside and gave her a bath, but the manager told me that they had a strict "no pets" policy and I couldn't keep her in my room. I didn't want to leave her, so I got a tent and slept in it with her, on the lawn of the hotel.

The next day, I took her to a vet, got her all her shots, got her dewormed, and had her treated for fleas. She stayed with me the whole time I was in Peru, then flew back to L.A. to live with me and Lux. I had her trained to become a service dog, and since then, she's been a constant companion, a huge positive in my life, and a subtle reminder of what I learned from that whole trip: Doing things you really don't want to for the right reasons can be rewarding, although sometimes not in the ways we expect. The same way I believe meditation plugs me into a special partnership with the universe, I believe the universe brought me and Wendy together as a celebration of doing the right thing. And yes, I understand that makes me sound like a total douche, especially to anybody who actually saw what an asshole I looked like on that show in Peru.

*   *   *

When I really analyze why I had refused to appear on *The Dudesons* in the first place, it's because I was operating with a mentality of scarcity. I worried that public attention and appreciation for people doing stupid shit was a limited resource. There wasn't enough of it to go around. If Jukka and *The Dudesons* were successful in that space doing stunts, pranks, and whatnot, there was less sustenance available for me, and that scared me.

When I relate this back to my own entry into the world of stand-up comedy, there were definitely people who had that same scarcity mindset about stand-up. I think about how I felt on Marc Maron's podcast when he was categorizing what I did as "not stand-up, per se" or how it pissed me off when Al Madrigal was taking shots at me. On some base level, I believe those guys feared that my stand-up might mean there was less space for them. I think about that in contrast to how someone like Joe Rogan has always welcomed me and others into stand-up. It doesn't mean that he has to like every other stand-up that comes along, but he doesn't feel like their success will take away from his. He operates with a mindset of abundance. There's enough out there for everyone. Granted, his podcast has turned him into a mogul and a very rich man. Perhaps it's easier to be generous when you're not struggling to survive. Or maybe his attitude of abundance is the very reason he's so rich in the first place. Then again, there are plenty of wealthy people who are greedy, selfish pricks, so go figure.

I must admit that, in my gut, I am much more like Maron than Rogan. My default position is to jealously defend my turf. But I don't want to be like that. It's selfish and, certainly in this case, unnecessary. The entertainment world is not just three channels of network TV anymore. It's not five hundred channels of cable TV. It's now a seemingly infinite universe of internet, streaming, social media, traditional television, films, live shows, and whatever else is just being invented as I write this sentence. There is genuine abundance out there. I don't need to be on guard against anyone encroaching on it. That was the attitude I took toward Zach "Zackass" Holmes. It was the attitude I took toward the other new cast members of *Jackass*. That doesn't mean that we don't still compete to create the best footage, but I don't look at their wins as my losses. There is no reason we all can't win together.

I've tried hard to extend that generosity to other hungry amateur Jackasses too. When I was on tour in Europe in 2016, I met these two Austrian kids who were incredibly creative with their stunts. They had created a game of Electric Twister, which was just like regular Twister except that every time you put a hand or foot down on a new color, you'd get an electric shock through the mat. It was pretty genius. They also did a simultaneous double nut-kick that I genuinely loved. I was impressed with their ingenuity, shared one of their videos, and stayed in touch with one of the two, a guy named Malte. A year or so later, he mentioned to me that he was collecting his pee in bottles, though he never told me his plans for it.

Cut to several years later, and I too had started collecting urine. I was maintaining a strict no-shitting policy in my podcast studio RV's bathroom. Then, when I saw this viral "condom challenge"—people were filling condoms with water and dropping them on each other's heads without breaking the condom—I pitched Tremaine the idea of trying it with a condom filled from my RV's sewage tank. He liked the idea, so we tried it over and over on the *Jackass* set, but we couldn't get it to work before we ran out of piss. I decided not to give up on the idea, and to make sure I didn't run out of piss the next time, we all started pissing into empty gallon jugs at my house. Even Lux got in on the act, with the help of a device called the GoGirl.

Soon enough, I came up with a better use for all this piss. I decided it would be awesome to set the world record for the highest belly flop ever done into pure urine. After all, it felt safe to say that nobody had ever done it before, so I was sure that whatever height I jumped from, I would be setting the record. I purchased the largest inflatable kiddie pool I could find, with a capacity of 134 gallons when filled to the "fill line."

We collected piss for months, and when one of my YouTube videos happened to mention that fact and show seventy or so jugs of it, I got an email from Malte accusing me of stealing his idea. I explained the origins of my urine collection regime and that it had nothing to do with him. When he emailed me back, I took one glance at his email and got pissed. He was still calling me a thief. I lost my patience and fired back that I did not take kindly to being accused of intellectual property theft. He was hardly the first guy in the world to collect urine anyway—Howard Hughes had done it long before either one of us—and that doing so hardly constituted a stunt idea in and of itself.

When I cooled off a little, I reread Malte's reply to my explanation and realized I had totally misinterpreted his response.

First off, English was not his first language, and something was getting lost in translation. When I read it more closely, I could see that he was actually trying to apologize for accusing me of stealing. I felt like shit that I'd blown up at him.

I was getting caught up in the whole scarcity mindset again. There was no reason to. I told him that instead of us fighting over this idea, let's do it together. I invited him to compete with me for that world record for the highest belly flop into urine. I shipped him two of the same exact kiddie pools I was using and sent photos of the way I had set mine up for practicing my belly flops. There would be nothing funnier than me attempting this stunt only to be easily bested by this random Austrian dude. And he was fucking stoked.

The thing is, I genuinely hadn't stolen Malte's idea. I didn't feel guilty about what I had done, and I didn't feel like I owed him anything. When he accused me, I got defensive and could easily have just dismissed him, blocked his email, and moved on with my life. But by inviting him to do this with me, I felt good about myself. Not only was there no cost to being kind and generous, it was a net benefit to me. It wasn't about who was right and who was wrong. This wasn't a zero-sum game. We could both win.

As it turned out, though, Malte didn't just best me in this contest—he fucking destroyed me. I was so terrified of doing my belly flop from the roof of my RV, I had been literally losing sleep. I had a paranoid fear of landing wrong and becoming paralyzed. On top of that, when I did it, I had to duct tape my hands behind my back to prevent myself from instinctually putting them in front of me to break my fall. Not only was there absolutely zero jump to my belly flop, I was so scared of taking the landing straight on my face and chest that I rotated somewhat in the air and landed mostly on my side. And keep in mind, my RV is only ten feet tall.

Malte, on the other hand, built a tower that was about fifteen feet tall and set his kiddie pool so ridiculously far from it that I thought he was joking with me when I first saw it. He didn't need to tie his hands behind his back; he had them outstretched like wings the whole way. He fucking flew, man. It was absolutely gorgeous.

* * *

I'd be lying if I tried to say that I wasn't neon green with jealousy of Malte's belly flop, and utterly ashamed of my own, but I still maintain that living in a mindset of abundance just makes you happier. Spiritually, I struggle with lots of shit—and anyone who has read this far will understand this—but the one area where I'd give myself a pretty good grade is my generosity. If someone does any work for me, I don't ever want them to feel taken advantage of. I will always lean toward overcompensating people. When I tour as a stand-up, I have what's called a "guarantee," which is basically what the promoter is paying me to show up. That guarantee is based on how many tickets they think they can sell. If I ever do a show that I know has underperformed sales-wise, I will tell my agent to refund the promoter whatever money they lost. That sort of defeats the purpose of a guarantee, but I don't want anyone to ever feel like they got a raw deal by being in business with me. On one level, I know that's also good business—that promoter won't hesitate to work with me again because he knows he's going to make money—but that's not the reason I do it. I do it because it's the bare minimum of what I need to do to feel okay about myself.

The fact is, I know I'm an insufferable douche. I'm self-centered, selfish, and narcissistic. I have to act with this sort of intentionality to fight against those impulses. And doing that makes me feel like a decent human being.

Even with these guardrails in place, I fuck up time and again. When I do, I beat myself up for it in a way that is usually out of proportion to whatever the fuckup actually was. Like, you know, climbing a mountain in Peru—and making twenty fucking You-Tube videos about it—because I didn't return a dude's phone call seven years earlier. On some level, I take a perverse pleasure in flaying myself for my fuckups, because that means I'm a moral, virtuous person. I have identified my failings and I will ritually flog myself for them so I and everyone around me knows what a moral, virtuous person I am. I guess there's an element of ethical grandstanding in all that, but so fucking what, if it makes me a better person?

While all this makes me sound like a swell guy, it's not really selfless. When I'm generous, when I hook someone up, when I overpay people for the work they do for me, I get to enjoy feeling like a great guy. I selfishly set aside a deliberate moment to bask in that feeling. When you think about it, there is almost something inherently selfish about being selfless because it genuinely makes you feel better about yourself. By that measure, doing good is actually its own reward: It *feels* good.

Not too long ago, Lux's dog, Olive, got into some chocolate in the middle of the night. We couldn't tell how much she had eaten, but we knew chocolate can be dangerous for dogs. It was about two in the morning, and Lux immediately started putting on her shoes to take Olive to the emergency vet clinic. I started to do the same.

"You don't need to go," she told me. "It's my dog. I'll take care of her."

"I want to go with you," I said. "I welcome this opportunity to be a great boyfriend." No kidding. I actually said that. I was already congratulating myself before even doing anything, which I suppose is par for the course for me. Even though I never thought Olive was in any real danger, and it was absolutely a pain in the ass to drive across town to the one vet that was open at two a.m., I believed it really would make Lux feel good about the kind of guy she was with. In turn, it would make me feel good about being that kind of guy. It was a win-win. Even if you're only living up to your ideals so you can pat yourself on the back for it, you're still living up to your ideals.

These are all just moments, but all of us are faced every day with countless small opportunities to prove ourselves to be the people we aspire to be. Every time we live up to that aspiration, it feels fucking good. You string together a bunch of those moments, and you've had a good day. You string together a few of those days, and you've had a good week. You keep stringing this stuff together, and I can't promise that you'll be happy, but you will almost certainly feel better than if you didn't.

*   *   *

My whole spiritual philosophy and my views on the universe were heavily shaped by a series of books called *Conversations with God*, written by an author named Neale Donald Walsch. Some people can't stomach those books because Walsch writes both parts of the conversation, his words and God's, which feels, if not blasphemous, at the very least a bit presumptuous. But for a guy like me who has never really subscribed to formal religion, none of that was a problem. Walsch's view is that we are all part of God, different pieces of the same divine life force, so why shouldn't he be able to write in God's voice? The core of his philosophy is that the best way to help yourself is by helping others: The selfishness of selflessness. I ate that shit up.

Back in 2018, I saw that Walsch was speaking at a conference in Chicago, so I booked tickets for me and Scott to go. After I'd made the arrangements, I realized that the same Saturday night of this conference, the UFC had a big pay-per-view event in Chicago. I fucking love UFC, so I reached out to UFC president Dana White on Instagram, and he totally hooked me and Scott up with tickets. Even then, the irony did not escape me that we were going to a conference to hear about the transformational power of love and oneness, and then going straight from there to watch people beat the ever-loving shit out of each other in a cage for money.

At this Celebrate Your Life conference, Scott and I stood out like two sore thumbs. Most of the people there were straight-laced-looking older women, but for as much as we didn't look like we belonged there, we totally did. During Walsch's talk, there was an extensive Q&A portion, which I was eager to participate in.

In *Conversations with God*, Walsch takes a pretty dim view on competition in general, essentially positing that highly evolved beings would never participate in activities where one being's victory is at the expense of another's defeat. I asked Walsch whether that meant that all competitive sports were inherently problematic.

"Not at all," he told me. "You're taking it a bit too literally. Of course it's okay to enjoy sports."

"Okay, that's good. But what about this: I'm going to an Ultimate Fighting event tonight to watch people try to hurt each other as much as they possibly can inside of a cage. Is that wrong?"

He laughed a little but shook his head. "Look, that's not something that I would be particularly into, but I imagine there's an art to it, the same way there is an art to boxing or baseball or any other sport. I don't think you need to beat yourself up about it." Essentially, his message to me was: *Lighten up, dude. It's not that serious.* None of us are monsters for not being able to live up to our highest ideals. Having those ideals to live up to and trying to again and again, knowing that you'll fail, is the best we can probably hope for.

* * *

Not long after I got sober, I got two small rescue dogs, Walter and Bernie. These dogs had both been deliberately abandoned because no one could handle them. Bernie is timid and meek. He's terrified of everything and deals with this fear by pissing all over the place. Walter is insanely fucking aggressive. He growls and barks at and tries to bite everyone he encounters in the world besides me. Actually, he even goes after me sometimes. He is completely resistant to training. When I got him, every doctor at the vet's office was unanimous in their opinion that Walter was beyond help and a genuine danger to humanity. They recommended he be put down. I got indignant when I heard that and vowed to prove those vets wrong.

They were not wrong. He has not mellowed at all. I've had him for more than twelve years now, and he's just as bad as the day I got him. Maybe worse. On more than one occasion, Lux has woken up in the middle of the night to Walter biting her so viciously that he's drawn blood. I don't have a close friend in my life whose blood he hasn't tasted. Anyone who gets anywhere close to me is in fucking danger from that dog.

Recently, I was at the end of my rope with him. I decided to take him back to the vets who first recommended that I put him down. I told them I was leaving him there for a couple days to be evaluated. I didn't want to be the one to make the decision, but if they thought he should be euthanized, I'd accept their decision. Essentially, I was hoping they'd make the hard call that I wasn't willing to and put us both out of our misery. But when I went back to pick him up, one of the vets told me, "You know, he seems better than last time." *No!* I couldn't believe it. They were not going to let me off the hook with Walter.

Not long after, I took Walter to another vet, in West Hollywood, and told them flat out, "He bites everyone, he's dangerous, I want you to put him down." They looked at me like I was a monster and told me that it's their policy not to euthanize dogs unless it's medically necessary. Foiled again. I know there are other vets who would certainly put Walter down, including a mobile unit that will come to our house to do the deed, and although I've considered that multiple times, I always get cold feet.

The thing about Walter, and to a lesser extent Bernie, is that symbolically, to me, they have always represented my sobriety and the amends I've had to make with the universe in order to maintain that sobriety. When I was still getting loaded, I was a fucking dangerous mess, just like those dogs, growling and snapping at people, pissing all over everything, sometimes literally. On some level, those dogs aren't just a reminder of that part of me, they are the dogs *I deserve*. The world had to deal with me at my worst for years, so now I've got to deal with them. Karma's a bitch. I can't put Walter down, because he represents a debt to the universe that I'm still paying off. Maybe one day I'll be able to, because I'll feel like that debt has been paid. Or maybe that debt will die of natural causes.

In fact, when I think about all three of those dogs—Walter, Bernie, and Wendy—they each seem to embody a different part of me: Wendy is the good, loving, generous part; Bernie is the frightful, fearful part; and Walter is the asshole. I've been trying to kill off the asshole inside of me, but if I'm being honest, much like with Walter, I haven't yet snuffed it out completely.

*   *   *

So let's get back to the question that opened this chapter: Am I happy? If I had to assess that honestly, my answer would be no. I know what you're thinking: Why did you wait until the end of this book to tell me that the guy dispensing wisdom throughout it is a miserable prick? Well, to be fair, I've told you in nearly every one of these chapters that I'm a miserable prick and that all my advice should be considered suspect.

I think what's more important than whether or not I'm happy is whether or not I'm okay with that. And I am. The thing is, I can truthfully say that I'm pretty much never at ease. I have some kind of default setting constantly telling me that I'm going to lose everything, so I better hurry up and work my ass off so that I'll be okay. It's like there's a fire under my ass that never goes out, which constantly compels me to strive for some type of achievement. When I ask myself whether I'd prefer to be a happy person or to be filled with anxiety but hustling my ass off to reach my goals, I'm proud to choose the hustle. To me, being happy means being content, and that seems like it will naturally lead to laziness. For me, words like "happy" and "content" feel like being done. And I'm not done. I still have a lot of shit I want to do.

The closest I get to happiness is thinking about a schedule filled with work and trips with my friends and plans for future projects I want to create and ideas for new businesses and blueprints for an animal sanctuary and a wedding to Lux. None of those things will bring me pure happiness as I define it, but they will inch me closer to it. To me, there is serenity in the hustle. I want to be perpetually striving for an accomplishment, even if that accomplishment just means coming up with a new way to shove something up my ass. I don't dream of a day far in the future when Lux and I will be quietly sitting on our porch, sipping iced tea and thinking of all the wonderful things we've done in our lives. I expect to be planning for the future and running toward it at full speed until the day when there is no future. I don't consider that a curse. To me, it's a gift.

But, hey, you may be different than me. Maybe you have the ability to stop and smell the roses without bloodying yourself among the thorns. But if there's something genuine that growing older has taught me, it's that you can't spend your life trying to become something you're not. I'm a fucking mess, I've got a lot of flaws, and it feels good to be working on them, but I'm not expecting to wake up one day having transformed myself into something entirely new. Change is certainly possible, but it's usually incremental. In other words, I just want to be the best version of that fucking mess that I can possibly be. I think that's a pretty good goal for anyone.

Look, life's big spoiler is that it ends the same way for all of us. Whether we put in the work to make ourselves better people, or whether we revel in being selfish dickheads, every one of us ends up finishing the game of life in the same position: horizontal. Sure, that sucks, but our journey in life is to figure out a way to be okay with that. To me, that's faith: The belief that everything's okay even when every fiber of my being tells me that it's not. I like to remind myself that the process of growing and improving that I'm putting myself through isn't about the final product, it's about the process itself. We're all fucked in the end, so what else is there?

In my high school yearbook when I was a senior, there was only one part of my senior quote that wasn't a reference to drugs or alcohol, and it read, "It's harder to climb up a hill than down, but the view is much better from the top." I don't know where that quote came from, but if I could, I'd add to it today. I know

now that life isn't really about making it to the top of that hill. None of us will ever reach that pinnacle of complete happiness, but climbing toward it feels a hell of a lot better than spending your whole life being the pussy standing at the bottom of the hill complaining about how fucking big and imposing it is.

So start climbing, motherfucker.

Acknowledgments

I have no idea how I got so lucky to have surrounded myself with such incredible and talented people, but without them I never would've been able to accomplish a fraction of what I have. Some of these people who I have to thank for the quality of life I enjoy today are Lux, Scott Randolph, Adam Ginivisian, Jeff Bernstein, Tommy Caudill, Mario Rivera, Paul Brisske, Sam Macaroni, Isaac Patterson, Leo Donati, Cordell Mansfield, Randy Stanger, my homegroup, my *Jackass* family, and, of course, my real family. I'm nobody without you guys. I love you all so much…

P.S.—The people who made this book happen fuckin' rule, too: David Peisner, Laura Nolan, and Brant Rumble!